In the Service of Life

In the Service of Life

A WICCAN PERSPECTIVE ON DEATH

Ashleen O'Gaea

CITADEL PRESS
Kensington Publishing Corp.
www.kensingtonbooks.com

CITADEL PRESS BOOKS are published by

Kensington Publishing Corp.
850 Third Avenue
New York, NY 10022

All Kensington titles, imprints, and distributed lines are available at special
quantity discounts for bulk purchases for sales promotions, premiums,
fund-raising, educational, or institutional use. Special book excerpts or
customized printings can also be created to fit specific needs. For details,
write or phone the office of the Kensington special sales manager:
Kensington Publishing Corp., 850 Third Avenue, New York, NY 10022,
attn: Special Sales Department, phone 1-800-221-2647.

First printing: April 2003

10 9 8 7 6 5 4 3 2 1

Printed in the United States of America

Library of Congress Control Number: 2002113467

ISBN 0-8065-2444-8

*This book is dedicated to
all the spirits living
in our work and in our memories.*

Contents

Preface

Practicing a religion that encourages, nay, *depends upon*, individualism, Witches write about Wicca from their own understanding and on their own terms. Though we all draw from the same well of lore and history, neo-Pagan religions all arrive at unique conclusions. Still, we have enough in common to share many religious customs and understandings.

How significant are the differences among Wiccan Traditions? Extremely . . . and not at all. To the extent that they empower us as individuals, focus our energies and ground us, they are essential, and to the extent that distinct Traditions act as poles among which our tributary energies course, powering our wider community, they are fundamental. They needn't be significant at all in terms of political or economic unity.

Valuing diversity, finding mutual strength in our combined energies, it makes sense to be clear about and accept the differences as well as the similarities in our various usages of language and custom. Here's some clarification of some of the usages in this book, so you won't have to wonder while you're reading.

I refer to and quote *The Charge of the Goddess* often because it is one of Wicca's most beautiful and significant pieces of liturgical material. The original version was written by Doreen Valiente for Gerald Gardner. I quote it sometimes from Janet and Stewart Farrar's book (see the Glossary) and sometimes from Adventure's *Book of Shadows*, which version has been slightly altered from the original. (Many *Trads* rewrite the Charge in their own terms, adding a line here and there, or leaving one out, depending on the Tradition's perspective and emphasis.)

You'll notice the pronoun *s/he*, which is meant to include male and female (when there is no easily understood "conglomerate" pronoun, *his* and *hers*, or *her* and *him* alternate). You'll see *God/dess*, when His or Her aspects are not the focus. Sometimes one gender or the other is used on purpose: if there's a reason, it will be revealed. I use the designations B.C.E. (*before common era*) and C.E. (*common era*) rather than *before Christ* and *anno Domini*. Furthermore, I have made up some words. Those that are not obvious in meaning are in the Glossary. As for *Wicca* and *Witchcraft*, my usage recognizes that all Wiccans are Witches but not all Witches are Wiccans.

Politics (from the Greek: "life of the community") has always been a manifestation of human interconnectedness; the match that lit the Burning Times was political; and we're *all* political, whether we know it or not. It's just that if you *do* know it, you don't have to be a pawn. Because so many people feel so much like pawns when someone's died, the occasional "political" opinion—mine— will be evident. Other Witches may well agree with me, but I'm only speaking for myself and from the perspective of the Adventure Tradition.

Because so many people come to Wicca from other religions, comparisons between Wicca and other religions are inevitable. It's also true that the "mainstream" tends to use Christianity's religious vocabulary when talking about religion in general. It can be confusing to use "Christian words" for another religion's ideas, without evoking the Christian images that dominate our culture's thoughts of death. To avoid as much of this confusion as possible, I'll point out and talk about differences in fundamental religious concepts when the vocabulary doesn't adequately reflect them.

Finally, I need and want to thank my family and my friends for their contributions to this book and for sharing the effort that went into writing it. Some of my perspectives changed over the years it took, and I am grateful to be part of a community which really *does* appreciate change and growth.

My HHP (Husband/High Priest) Canyondancer and our son the Explorer kept the home fires burning whilst I sequestered myself in the back room to write this book, and that means as much to me as if I'd felt the Goddess's own hand reassuringly on my shoulder all those months. I am especially grateful to Chris (Grianwydd), who has, more than anyone I know, always been able to forge grace from turmoil, whose patience and trust are unequaled, and who has been my sister-friend for a lot longer than half my life.

This preface would end here, except that there are readers interested in perspectives on death, but unfamiliar with the religion of Wicca. Even Wiccan and other neo-Pagan readers need to know how this book understands Wicca. For all readers, then, here's a brief primer.

Wicca's not the only Western neo-Pagan religion, but it's the best known. Formalized by Gerald Gardner in the mid-twentieth century, Wicca knows and cherishes the cycles of Nature: sun-up, sun-down, birth-growth-death-rebirth. Earth's solar and lunar cycles symbolize *all* the cycles that move the Universe, and in ritual observance of solar and lunar holidays, Witches revere life's interconnectedness. Wiccans celebrate eight solar holidays in the year, called Sabbats, including Halloween and May Day. (Yes, we really do dance the May Pole.) We also follow the Moon's cycle, meeting at Esbats to celebrate the full and new Moons.

Witches worship "the Dance of Life." In Circles, Witches invoke the Goddess and Her Horned Consort. Our Horned God is the game that dies so that the hunter's tribe can live; He is also the grain that falls in harvest to rise again in new crops. Our God dies and is reborn in *all* the natural cycles; and our Goddess is life's womb and the cycles into which we are all born and reborn. Like our God, our Goddess has many aspects. She is Maiden, Mother, and Crone; She is creation and destruction. The Goddess and the God

The Wheel of the Year

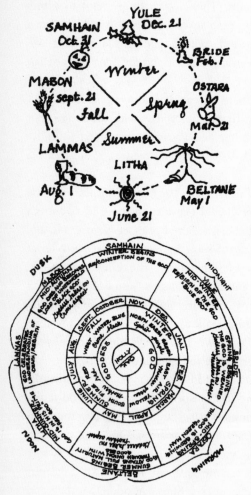

The Wheel of the Year is Wicca's liturgical calendar, marking the eight Sabbats Wiccans (and other neo-Pagans) celebrate during the year.

Both illustrations are from Campsight Coven's *Book of Shadows,* and agree with and incorporate correspondences from various sources. Most covens and Traditions develop their own versions of this religious calendar; some include the new and dark Moons, and additional symbols according to the coven's or Tradition's interests and focus.

Top: a simple version of the Wheel of the Year, Wicca's liturgical calendar, showing the dates of Wicca's eight Sabbats, and their relationship to the four seasons.

Bottom: a more elaborate version of the Wheel, showing the Sabbats corresponding to the Elements and Directions as well as to other symbols.

have different names in different cultures and in each season, but Their dance—and ours—is always the Dance of Life.

Witches aren't devil-worshipers. Wicca draws on pre-Christian traditions, asserting cooperative human nature and complimentary universal energies. Absolute opposition is not an element in Wiccan *thealogy* (see Glossary), nor does Wicca hold that there is any supernatural realm from which our lives can be directed. Satan, like Jehovah, is a Judeo-Christian-Islamic concept, and plays no part in Wiccan thealogy. Some Satanists and some troubled folk immersed in abuse still call themselves "Witches," but they're not Wiccan. Satanists accept a Christian description of the world and choose to resist what they see as its spiritual oppression, symbolizing their resistance with images of the Christian devil.

Christianity has not always felt threatened by Witchcraft, but when the Church was corrupt in the Middle Ages, Paganism *was* a threat to the Church's *political* control of Europe. European Paganism was pretty well wiped out before the Inquisition was declared. Though today's Wiccans are very different from classical Witches, the vilification we've inherited began as a political exploitation of ignorance and fear, and it still is.

Happily, it's been a long time since I was asked, but for the record, I'll answer anyway: The only blood sacrifices Wiccans make . . . are at the blood bank. Our God offers Himself to us in game and grain (and in the rising and setting of the Sun, and in the season-making orbit of our planet, etc.). We, with our God, will be reborn through the Goddess, for She is all that is generative and eternal, while He is all that dies and is reborn. Witches honor the God's death in the service of life, and celebrate our participation in the cycles of life, by offering back to the Gods a portion of cere-monial meals. A song, home-made cookies, a wreath woven of flowers, or a life-changing promise is the sort of thing a Witch offers to the Gods.

When a small group of Witches—a coven—meets to work, individuals' energies are focused in ritual and collective energy is directed, released and grounded. A solitary works in the same way; and solitary or with covens, Wiccans work to heal, to soothe souls, to encourage success, and to oppose harm. The understanding that guides our work is that the energy we send out returns to us threefold; not wanting to reap misery, we don't sow it. A Witch's work is always respectful of life. Orgies and street drugs are *not* part of Wiccan worship. Wicca holds the creative power of sex sacred, and Witches invoke this energy symbolically in ritual. Witches take a reputation as herbalists and healers seriously, and make no abuse of drugs.

An ye harm none, do as ye will is Wiccan law. Witches pay more attention to *harm none* than to *as ye will*. Practicing the Craft balances us, keeping our lives in harmony with the Life we all share. Recreated from the Inquisition's ashes, Wicca glows with the spirit of humanity's first religion and carries on meeting humanity's religious needs today.

Spring 2002 C.E.

In the Service of Life

In the Cycles of the Planet

Music and lyrics by Ashleen O'Gaea

In the cy - cles of the pla - net dwell our hu - man lives and spir - its; in the pat - terns of the wa - ter, in the rhy - thms of the Sun. In the air that we are breath-ing hangs the sto - ry of our fu - ture; in the heart - beat of the Earth, we hear the course our lives will run.__ And for all the spir-its liv-ing in our work and in our memories we ga-ther now to sing the songs of dark-ness and of light.__ For those who've gone be - fore __ us, ah, we sing of how we miss them, and for those who've yet to join us, we sing wel-com- ing to - night.__

Transcribed by Sylvia Lau McDonald

Introduction

Was it always like this? The dying curtained off, sometimes miles away from loved ones, the dead prepared for burial by strangers, the survivors trying not to cry and wishing they didn't have to be there at the funeral?

No, it wasn't. *And it doesn't have to be now.*

How do we know that death hasn't always been the foreign and terrifying event it is today? We know because those for whom it wasn't have left us their records.

The hunters' priest, draped in the skin and horns of the game his tribe kills, stares at us still from the walls of Lascaux's cave;[1] and the grains of fossilized pollen, all that remain of the flowers that covered a fetally folded body, are still present in Iran's prehistoric cemeteries.[2]

Lascaux's priest confides to us that the hunted animals' life forces had his respect and were sacred. We know from more recent

[1]Les Trois Frères (*Lay Twa Frehr*) is a cave on the north side of the Pyrenees, about 20 miles south of Toulouse, France. The Sorcerer, as the 2½-foot-tall image is called, dominates his chamber from 15 feet above its floor. The sacred engraved or drawn figures here are about 30,000 years old. He "may have been" a shaman. John Putman, "The Search for Modern Humans," in *National Geographic Magazine* (October 1988).

[2]At the Shanidar Cave in what is now Iran, this example is known as Shanidar IV, "the flower burial." Sixty thousand years ago, the body was carefully positioned to face west. At least eight kinds of flowers were offered at this grave; seven of them are still used medicinally today in Iran and beyond. Joseph Campbell, *Historical Atlas of World Mythology*, vol. I, pt. I.

tribal experience[3] that the ritual surrounding the hunt was as much to ensure the game's rebirth as to ensure its death in the service of the hunting clan's life.

We know that mourners at the grave now known as Shanidar I accepted the sanctity of every life, for their loved one was a cripple who had survived only with kinfolks' help.[4] We know that their understanding was of the grave as womb, for the body was carefully positioned like a fetus, ready to be reborn. "Funerals" in those days, quite likely, included sympathetic magical workings toward rebirth. This expectation of rebirth was reinforced by the flowers the gathered clan threw into the grave. That flowers die in one season and return in another did not escape them.

Wicca descends from that primal understanding of human life as moving through nature's cycles of life and death in close kinship with other species *and* in relationship with the landscape and environment, which is also shaped by those cycles. But because the civil laws under which we live today were written from a perspective of human *apartness from* nature, death is no longer integral to our experience of life. That idea, that human virtue resides in our *distance* from nature, has moved us to get as far away from death as we can. Death reminds us that we're *part* of nature, and mortal. And because now we're unfamiliar with it, it's easy to be scared of death, and many of us are.

It would be possible to write a hundred *more* books exploring the development of these circumstances, but none of us needs a

---

[3] The North American plains' Mandan tribe's Buffalo dance is a ritual that reanimates the great beast symbolically with its willing death as game; less than 100 years ago the Penobscots on North America's east coast turned out in antlered headdresses for the stags who were their partners in the spiral dance. Raymond Buckland, *Buckland's Complete Book of Witchcraft* (Llewellyn Publications, St. Paul, 1986).

[4] According to Joseph Campbell in volume I of the *Historical Atlas*, the one-armed male in this grave was evidently killed by falling rocks about 42,000 years ago. John Putnam's article in *National Geographic* mentions 11,500 year-old "Romito 2," found in an Italian cave. A dwarf who died a cripple at the age of 17, "Romito" was entirely dependent upon a community founded in compassionate cooperation. Campbell's work, too, supports our image of a paleolithic perception of one-ness with each other (and the rest of life).

book to tell us that we need to reintegrate death into our conscious cosmology. *What we need to understand is that death has always been sad, and challenging, too; but it* hasn't *always been frightening. It will always be sad, but it doesn't ever have to be scary again.*

We used to have greater control over it than we do now, and we will again as we look to our spiritual heritage. No, our paleo-ancestors couldn't *prevent* death. But they *could*—and did—confront it directly, sitting together till death overcame the elderly or wounded or ailing; preparing the body of a parent, a child, a lover, or a friend for burial; mourning communally and ritually re-entering public life with the help of loving friends, who did not pretend that nothing had happened.

In this sense, death was *celebrated* in the old days, and in some Western cultures[5] there is still an element of celebration in the rites that attend death.[6] But for most of us, death is still a medieval specter from which we prefer to look away, and for most people, it's still an achievement to get through the funeral without showing any emotion.

This is not a healthy approach. The problems that denied grief can cause in a human body and mind are well documented.[7] Luckily, this post-Victorian attitude is not a mandatory approach, and

[5]This book is about death from a Wiccan perspective, and Wicca is a Western faith. Its roots are, loosely speaking, Anglo-Celtic. There are other neo-Pagan traditions in the world which are equally sensitive, and if there aren't books about those perspectives on death, there should be.

[6]Although according to Robert E. Kavanaugh in his 1972 Penguin Books release, *Facing Death*, Irish waking is today seriously dysfunctional, it is still a remnant of a community-affirming feast at which the deceased is given a new role in relationship to the survivors. In Audrey Gordon's essay "The Jewish View of Death: Guidelines for Mourning," part of Elisabeth Kübler-Ross's 1975 Touchstone (Simon & Schuster) book, *Death, the Final Stage of Growth*, the re/integrating traditions of Hallacha, Shiva, and Kriyah take a different tone but achieve the same result.

[7]John Bradshaw, *Homecoming: Reclaiming and Championing Your Inner Child* (Bantam Books, New York, 1990). (This book suggests ways to heal the "dis-ease" caused by our wide range of unresolved griefs. I recommend it for everybody.) Also two books by Elisabeth Kübler-Ross: *Death, the Final Stage of Growth* (Touchstone Books, Simon & Schuster, New York, 1975) and *On Death and Dying* (Collier Books, MacMillan, New York, 1969).

not the only way a human brain can apprehend and appreciate—yes, appreciate—death.

This book explores another conceptual framework, a Wiccan perspective on death. This book is for Wiccan clergy, for students of religion, for Witches and other Pagans trying to sort through their ideas, and for non-Wiccans who are interested in some of real Witchcraft's real thinking.

We feel each other's strength through time and space when we consider death, even though we speak of it in different tongues and metaphors. We reach out to each other, undaunted by the passage of miles and years. And whether we draw upon Northern shamanistic[8] and Eastern transcendent experiences or those that the Western traditions have to offer, Witches everywhere are united in the quest to pass through the Gates[9] with dignity, in perfect love and perfect trust.

Furthermore, Wicca challenges us to deal with deaths of many kinds. A passage commonly used in Initiations reads, "There are two deaths by which we die, the greater and the lesser. These are the death of the body and the death of Initiation, and of these two, the death of the body is the lesser." (This is an adaptation of passages in the *Egyptian Book of the Dead*.)

Even when they do not recreate death and rebirth, most Wiccan rituals allude to it. So death is not entirely unfamiliar to Wiccans, nor so terrifying as it can be to followers of other faiths. As another initiatory passage from the same source reveals to us, "But to be reborn you must die, and to die you must be born, and

---

[8]We need to acknowledge the distinction between shamanic religions—like North American Indians'—and shaman*istic* religions—like Wicca, although Wiccan cosmology is in some ways similar to shamanic views of the world. Wicca is not shamanic but *shamanistic* in those respects. Most of us borrow some bits and phrases from shamanic religions and experience, but our tradition is about shared experience and direct transaction with Gods and spirits, and there are other significant differences as well.

[9]"Passing through the Gates" means dying. Witches use this metaphor to imply that beyond physical death there are other realms where life, albeit in different form, goes on.

without love you may not be born; and this is all the magic."
Wiccan perspectives on death are magical.

Whether you are Wiccan or not, you will find some thoughts of
comfort in this book. And you will find that those comforting
thoughts and information are not confined to category and chapter but weave in and out of every section, popping up in different
contexts, because taken on their own terms, Life and Death pop
up in different contexts.

Because each of us learns and understands in many different
ways, *In the Service of Life* talks about death in many different ways.
Starhawk (and most everybody else) calls life a spiral dance, and
this book is about one of the dance steps, death. The aspects of
death we need to talk about aren't isolated in clear-cut chapters
because our experience isn't isolated: death is interconnected with
the rest of life, and this exploration of Wicca's perspectives on
death reflects that interconnection.

Our commonly accepted dread of death is not the only
approach or response of which we're capable. I write about Wicca's
perspective for two reasons: first, I am Wiccan; and second, in this
respect Wicca is as fearless, dreadless a religion as you could hope
to find. It troubled me greatly when Derek Humphrey's book
Final Exit[10] was reviewed and discussed on all the weekend afternoon PBS shows for two or three weeks (back in 1991) and the
only perspective the speakers took was monotheistic. For all the
hurting people stuck in the tortuous territory of *either/or* thinking,
damned if they do and damned if they don't, I wanted to weep.
But writing a book about Wicca's perspectives on death seemed
more practical.

And this book is practical. This book integrates the spiritual
with the practical because *Wicca* integrates the spiritual and the
practical. When an activity is spiritual, is done with spiritual intent,
then even the most mundane part of it is holy. Thus, when we are

---

[10]Derek Humphrey, *Final Exit* (The Hemlock Society, Los Angeles, 1991).

in the presence of death, nothing we do is ordinary, not even the ordinary things. Everything we do is magical.

In a way, this book is a work of magic. As a Witch, I work magic all the time; every time, in fact, that I act *with intent*. By putting these words to paper and sharing them with you, I hope to enchant the world just a little bit. I hope to remind the world— that's you, Reader—that there are magical perspectives on life *and* on death. Wicca's is a magical perspective on death, and here I hope to share one understanding of it with you. Blesséd be.

PART ONE

From earliest times, humans have approached death in a sort of reciprocal way. Understanding, for instance, that life feeds on life, ancient cultures gathered food reverently, often leaving something—a drop of blood, a libation of wine, seeds for next year's crop—in exchange for the plant or animal life taken. This reciprocity undoubtedly extended to mineral lives when stones were chosen for shamans' and magicians' pockets and pouches.

It's more than obvious that we have a "relationship" with death: always have had, always will. Death is inevitable for us mortals, and unpleasant as modern societies can make it, our encounters with death don't have to be as horrid as they usually are these days.

Neither do a lot of our *other* relationships. Most famously, marriages and parent–child relationships have soured in their stereotypes, but those relationships are being reclaimed, restructured, reborn. It's important to understand that Wicca gives us guidelines for recreating our relationships with death, too.

Death has been closeted relatively recently, since the beginning of the twentieth century; but that's long enough for many of us to have lived our whole lives, so far, without ever approaching death as natural. It *is* natural, though, and like anything else natural, it's intimately connected with lots of other things. We usually call those other things Life.

In Part One of this book, we'll look at death from the Goddess's perspective. She is Life—all that is eternal and generative. Though She does not die, She nonetheless faces death. Looking at Her comportment, studying what She teaches us in Wicca's liturgies, we can find inspiration and direction for those times when we are survivors of death and loss.

"Beyond death, I give you peace, and freedom, and reunion." So says the Goddess to us in Her charge. In *this* life we are beyond death, and in Part One of this book we'll look at the ways we can find peace, and freedom, and reunion here and now.

Death and the Goddess

And as She descended through the Realms
and leaving Her robes and gems behind Her
on the harrowing trail,
She came at last before the Lord of the Underworld,
and She was bound and blindfolded
as though She had no body
and no senses left
by which to perceive.
And before the Lord of the Underworld
She knelt and said,
"I have set aside all My clothes and jewelry
and come before You bringing nothing;
and I kneel before You
not because I love You, but to ask You
why You cause all I love
to wither and die."
And the Lord of the Underworld embraced Her most tenderly
* and said,*
"It is age and fate, Lady,
against which I am helpless;
but when all things die, I give them rest
and strength that they may be born again,
as I am reborn through Your life."

The Goddess comes by Her command of death honestly, by virtue of Her descent to the Underworld and Her submission to the God. The Goddess does not die there, for the Goddess is eternal; yet She accepted Death's challenge in Her own way. Between Them, the whole range of relationships to Death is manifest.

The Goddess does not die, but She gives birth to that which dies, and so She grieves. In this grief She submits to the death of Her uncorrupted joy. When She ascends from the Underworld She and Her joy are reborn from the depths of Her Self. Because the Goddess represents all that is eternal and generative, we sometimes forget that Her adventures through the Lands of Death are as courageous and faith-affirming as the God's. The God faces death and rebirth every year. The Goddess faces loss and restoration, and Her example can inspire us as well.

We really can begin to find again, in our ordinary lives, the elements of heroic adventure. Love and Death. The light and dark twins. There's not been a heroic story in the history of the world that isn't about love or death, and most of them incorporate both. The mythic aspects of love can get lost in these crude and anxious days; but the mythic aspects of death still materialize easily.

This makes the several days following a death and any funerary rituals a *magical* time, when significant workings can be accomplished. Family relationships can be mended, perspectives re-evaluated, and new attitudes taken. The veil between the Worlds is thin around people who are touched by death.

After the death of someone close to you, your usual behavior and ways of thinking tend to be suspended. It's almost as if some other consciousness has taken over. It has. It is a primal consciousness, and it radiates from the experiences of birth and death and other passages. It charges us, and we can use this energy for the daunting mundane tasks which face a family and friends when someone dies. But She charges us with a non-ordinary energy, too, and we can use that as a magical tool to work emotional wonders.

Many Pagans strive to "live mythically," as Joseph Campbell dubbed it. From this perspective we see these mortal, seventy-or-so-year incarnations of ours as forays into legendary landscapes, adventures, quests.[1] Too often, our mundane lives, where we make our living, demand that we take a less inspiring perspective. And too often, it takes something as powerful as a death to give us a shiver of memory that it was not always this dull and meaningless.

It's not unusual, when you're taking care of things after some-one has died, to feel as though you're on a mission or a quest. Of course, you are. Your mission may be to make sure the dearly departed is bid an appropriate farewell; your quest may be to con-tinue a project that was left unfinished. Any commitment you make under these circumstances should be serious, because it will be an identification with whoever has died. It's both a pledge to carry the memory and a sort of chest-pounding assertion of will-ingness to face your own mortality.

This is one of the ways that death is transformed to life. Not only can *you* be reborn, redefined, recharged, and redirected when you face the death of someone close; but something else—a pro-ject, a donation, a venture, a change of mind or heart—might come of the changes you undergo. This "death energy" is not uncontrollable. If we choose to do so, we can direct this energy, ritually or materially, ground our feelings, change our world.

Although our physical experience of death could be taken for an end, it is actually a moment of conception for our birth into Wholeness.[2] Everyone's seen the poem reprinted in *Dear Abby*, the one about the sails: *you* see them disappearing through your tears,

---

[1]In the *Creative Mythology* volume of *The Masks of God*, Joseph Campbell talks about Arthur's knights each entering the woods where they perceived them to be the thickest, for through the thickest wood lies the best adventure; perhaps this explains our "choices" to be born into the families we were, if nothing else explains them.

[2]Different cultures consider this in different time frames. The *Tibetan Book of the Dead* suggests a seven-day journey; some Western experiences suggest one that takes a matter of hours. In any case, time is not foremost in the consciousness of Passing Through, and is only measured from the perspective of those staying on this plane.

while for the folks waiting on the other shore they're just *appear-ing* over the horizon; it's like that.

That other shore is Summerland's shore, we say; and "sailing away," especially to the West, is a common metaphor for death in many cultures. One sails away to the afterlife, the other shore, through the straits of the Underworld, guided by the God, who has navigated the currents safely many times before. These images are certainly good ones to carry, and consistent with Wicca's historical and ethnic origins. By themselves, though, they're inadequate to express Wicca's understanding of death. Our culture focuses all too closely on *this* side of death, but unilateral understandings are antithetical to Witchcraft. There is no sailing away without some sailing toward; there is no sailing away without some sailing back.

Marine metaphors come easily to Wicca, for it comes from shores and islands, and knows the sea as Mother. Tidal imagery permeates much of Witchcraft's liturgical material; Water, with the other elements, is honored in every rite. Waters fill wombs; the Sea is a womb. If dying from this life is called sailing away,[3] then birth might be called sailing back.

"As above, so below." None of the seas' shipping lanes have ONE WAY ↑ buoys anchored anywhere, and the cosmic seas on all the planes are sailed from "both" shores, too. And all the time we are sailing toward Oneness and Individuality. As sea tides flow below, so tides of longing flow above (within).

Longing. This is the "desire" of which the Goddess speaks in Her Charge, when She tells us, "I am that which is achieved at the end of all desire." She is that which we achieve when the longing is ended—by fulfillment, not extinction. We *achieve* Her. Her Wholeness is our goal. She is both the alchemical result of longing satisfied *and* the alchemical element by which the longing is satisfied.

---

[3]My dad fished much of his life, in boats he built himself, off the Oregon coast. When he found out he was dying, he said, "Looks like I'd better design one more ship."

In Starhawk's Creation myth[4] the God, once aware of Himself as separate from His Mother, ever seeks to return to Her. "But always desire draws Him back toward the Goddess." We have always known this. The most ancient shamans understood a very complex relationship between life and death. They understood it in analogies to the game animals that gave their mortal lives to nourish the hunter's tribe, animals they ritually sang back to flesh and bone again. They expressed it in flower burials and with grave goods; and in ritual they reiterated it at every season.

Our modern understanding of this relationship has forgotten, however, that if the buffalo was willing to die to the hunter's arrow only on condition of being sung back to life, then being alive must be of *value*. And we, like the buffalo, are drawn toward rebirth into Individuality as strongly as we're drawn to reunion with the Whole.

The tension between Wholeness in the Mother and the indescribable delight and variety of experiences possible to those of the incarnate persuasion would be meaningless if each pole weren't equally compelling. In other words (and this, of course, is what "makes it go") the Goddess wants to be individually conscious beings as much as individual beings—i.e., the God—want to be One again. We describe this compulsion (or propulsion) as a longing to re-experience the Whole: She is "that which is attained at the end of all desire." She fulfills the Longing. It must be the case that the Whole also longs for Individual experience. Otherwise, "Nirvana" achieved, life as we know it would cease to exist. Life pulses on, though, so we can rest easy that the Longing is reciprocal.

The Longing can be satisfied, in a way, on the physical level: we can love, and thus become the one that is more than one. The Great Rite sanctifies love on every plane, so we know that pleasure is holy. Knowing that there is more to us than meets the eye or

---

[4] *The Spiral Dance* (Harper & Row softcover, 1979), 17.

weights the hand, we know that sex isn't the only worshipful pleasure; but neither are any expressions of love offensive to the Goddess. More than underscoring the Goddess's promise that "all acts of
love and pleasure are My rituals," being able to satisfy the Longing
here and now in our relationships with each other is an affirmation,
a sign that we'll be able to satisfy the desire to be Whole again, too.

So the Longing does not give us pain, it *carries* us. It is an
energy beyond our own. We all feel it. Some of us recognize it as
spiritual, some of us don't, but we all feel it. It's in the will to live,
for this is the nature of this force—*the* force—this Longing. The
force is not either of the poles but the cycling between them, and
it is not an inherently sorrowful journey but inherently joyous.
Everything we call love is some variation on this theme. We, dying
and reborn like our God, are a variation on this theme.

Wicca, for all the popular (and stereotypical) images of magickal[5] wars and evil spells, is not vengeful. That is, we do not
acknowledge a whimsical Goddess who takes offense and strikes
back. She doesn't hurt us or scare us, so we don't hurt or scare
other people to follow Her example. The Goddess we acknowledge is the Creative Void, the Cauldron, the Grail, the Womb.

Ah, the womb, death's other side. Death is painful; birth is
painful. Understanding why *birth* is painful may shed some light on
death's pain. Birth is painful because we have cerebral cortexes,
which make our heads bigger than other mammals' heads. Birthing
our big-headed babies stretches us wider. Two things mitigate that
pain (which, I have heard,[6] is the greatest pain a body can actually
feel). One is the brain's beta endorphins, and the other is the
knowledge that something incredibly wonderful and exponentially
worth it is happening.

---

[5]Spelling it *magick* implies some ceremonialism, which is part of the popular image of
Witches as magicians. Many Pagan writers use this spelling when we want to invoke, refer
to, or acknowledge the "Sorcerer's Apprentice" model.

[6]I heard this from my midwives as I was giving birth to the Explorer on the floor in the
bedroom. I believed them. I still do.

We can feel physical pain when people we care about die. It's as if they have to be disentangled from our nervous system, like pulling a vine off a fence. We have our beta endorphins, but we don't have much sense that something *good* is happening.

But something good *is* happening, something incredibly wonderful and "exponentially worth it" *is* happening. Someone we loved and laughed and cried with, someone we will miss forever, is being Whole. It is what we all Long for, the Wholeness we leave when we are born. (It may also be true that someone we loved is finally free of considerable pain, which is another good thing.)

Think for a moment of the newborn human child. There s/he is, curled up comfortably in this wonderful warm, dark, soothing place, and the next thing s/he knows, rough and tumble s/he's squeezing down the birth canal, buffeted, advanced, repelled, pushed and pulled for hours. Can't hear the heartbeat very clearly now, and it's not very comfortable or soothing. And when s/he's out, it's like coming through a wall, and then suddenly it's light and cold and loud and tactile, the movement is erratic, and there's pokey things! Suddenly, too, there's hunger and intestinal activity, and lungs and hard mattresses. If the kid is lucky, eventually there's a warm embrace, a heartbeat again, and a breast, but there's no guarantee.

Meantime, we're "ooohing" and "awwwwing" and talking in little voices and generally going gaga over those little tiny fingers and those perfect little toes. We think a baby's just the dandiest darn thing ever to come down the pike, but that might not be the way the baby'd describe it. Just so, we tend to think that death's the worst darn thing ever to come down the pike—but that might not be the way the dead would describe it. In fact, most people who report near death experiences report that they'll never be scared of death again.[7]

---

[7]See Elisabeth Kübler-Ross, *On Death and Dying*, and Raymond Moody's *Life After Life* for more about this.

The Goddess's experience of death is through the God's mortality. She knows the loss of child and mate; Hers are the original losses. Her Charge gives us some understanding of Her bearing of this reality, and thus some guidance (which is why, of course, it's called a "charge"). She is Life, so our worship of Her guides our approach to life—and death.

We like to be in control of our approach, but sometimes we confuse control with suppression, because that's mostly what we've been taught to do. And of course, suppressing feelings long enough makes you feel as though they're bad feelings you shouldn't admit to having; so when they escape, out of control, you can feel pretty bad about it. It is not uncommon for such a thing to happen at a funeral.

Sometimes people sob uncontrollably. This is the stereotypical expectation, and it has a long history of social acceptance. But sometimes when you're in the middle of coping with a death in your community—your immediate family, your coven, or among your cowan friends or in wider circles, a *joke* slips out. A really horrible pun, dreadfully macabre.

When that happens, it's easy to feel embarrassed, even guilty, because society tends to take death jokes at a funeral as disrespectful. Yet, "Let there be beauty and strength . . . and mirth and reverence with you," the Goddess charges us. So are jokes really all that inappropriate?

Well, no, they're not. At least not always.

Jokes—words and gestures, "mirth," the Goddess says—are okay for several reasons. First, they break the tension. When somebody dies, your body goes into crisis mode. There's a lot to do, not a lot of time to do it. It's all important and you feel as though if you make any mistakes, disaster will follow. There's a *lot* of pressure, and jokes can be a life-saving valve through which to release some of it.

Jokes also remind us that we are still alive, that our perspective on the world is only temporarily narrowed and dimmed, and that we will, presently, see the world as a gay and sunny place again.

Even if the joke is morbid (and it probably is), if it makes you smile, that muscular movement will generate subtle changes in brain chemistry that will eventually help you find your way back to balance.

When a co-worker's mother died, she told me, a family friend who was thought to have known about the death suggested that someone make a call to Mom to tell her some news. My co-worker responded that "it'd be a hell of a long-distance charge." Even though lines like that may make their speakers lower their heads immediately, they're *good* jokes in that they help to keep the world balanced for the bereaved.

And who hasn't made a rude joke or two when mail comes for someone who's been dead for quite some time? At another office where I worked, we got catalogues for a member of the boss's family who died several years ago. Seeing something in them that this woman might have liked, we were known to wonder aloud how to calculate the shipping charges.

If you have ever felt bad (in any sense) for cracking a joke at a funeral, or about a funeral, take a moment right now to think about that. (I'm talking about little private and whispered jokes, not disruptive outbursts.) When it's *your* funeral, when *your* friends are gathered, how do you want them to act in *your* memory? Do you hope they will be dour and tearful? Or would you rather they remembered you in celebration? I know that in my own case, it would be both disappointing and unfitting if nobody cracked wise when I die—providing that their jokes aren't *too* much better than mine have been.

It seems to be part of the common psychological knowledge now that jokes can express feelings that would be overwhelming, even to the point of rejection, if we expressed them in full seriousness. Few things are more overwhelming than death, so a lot of talk about it is, or at least attempts to be, humorous.

Laughter can't take the place of tears, of course, nor should it. Rather, laughter should take its place *alongside* tears in the celebration of life's transformations. If births can move us to tears, then it's alright for death to move us to laughter. Sadness, fear, and anger are the feelings that *most* need to be aired and acknowledged because they are the feelings that can do us the most harm if they are suppressed or denied.

When Canyondancer's mother died of a massive heart attack, much was unresolved. The funeral was held on a Saturday, and after the service was over and all the mourners had left the house, we collapsed and turned on the television set, looking for something easy to watch till we could relax enough to sleep. What we tuned in was *Saturday Night Live*, in its first or second year. Decked in an undertakerly suit and sinister dark glasses, a "Mr. Mike" told warped versions of well-known children's stories.

The night we tuned in? The Little Engine that Could puffed up the hill chanting, "Heart attack, heart attack, I left my pills in the round-house, I left my pills in the round-house." Well, 'dancer and his two brothers just fell over, literally, and laughed till they wept. Against their example, there was no way I could keep from laughing, although I was appalled. Looking back, I think it was just what we all needed. Several years later, we were able to appreciate then and there the laughter that rang out at my father's memorial service (about his determination to win at tennis, even against much younger players).

The common sensibility that we ought to speak in whispers and ever-so-solemnly about death comes from a perception of death as a punishment and its association with Judgments of Doom. These ideas developed, in turn, from the concept of original sin, which Wiccan thealogy does not include.

If you believe that human nature is inherently sinful, i.e., by nature at least disappointing to deity, then you are quite naturally going to worry about how that deity will judge you. But Wiccans are without that belief, and do not fear the Gods or worry that Their love is at all conditional. It is virtually impossible for Wiccans to accept the idea of original sin. In the Christian explanation, Eve's original sin was partaking of "forbidden" knowledge, of self-awareness; but Witches hold self-awareness sacred. How else are we to know that we are God/dess?

Carl Sagan suggests in *Dragons of Eden*[8] that the reason humans suffer pain in childbirth *is* related to our seizure of knowledge: our cerebral cortex enlarges our heads, giving us a tighter squeeze through the birth canal, which, not much enlarged from our *Dream-time* (our prehistoric golden age), must stretch when we give birth. Scientists like to say that the simplest explanation of any phenomenon is the preferred explanation (the principle of parsimony), and Wicca tends to agree. With such a straightforward explanation of childbirth's pain (which is different for each of us, of course), we have no need to relate that experience to a jealous, vengeful god's retribution.

Birth hurts because it stretches us. We're the only animal capable of letting it stretch us more than physically, letting it stretch us psychologically and emotionally as well. Might not the hurt of death be the same thing, expanding us? Might the pain of death be a growing pain?

The Explorer was born at home on the bedroom floor after 12 hours of vigorous labor which completely exhausted me—and all of that energy was a *very* small offering to make compared to the honor of participating in that event. Likewise, the energy that Canyondancer and I put into parenting is a small price to pay to be part of this person-who-is-our-son's life. There's always a price, and that's a description, not a threat. One of Wicca's protocols is that you never haggle over the price of a magical tool, and life's a magical tool.

Wiccans interpret death similarly. I think you could say that death corresponds, roughly, to a fetus's "dropping" and turning to properly face the birth canal. The dropping and turning aren't part

---

[8] Carl Sagan, *The Dragons of Eden: Speculations on the Evolution of Human Intelligence* (Random House, New York, 1977).

of the birth process *per se*, and you don't call the midwife yet; but these things must happen before a birth can proceed. When we die from this world, this plane, it leaves us "dropped" and "turned" so that we can properly face the *rebirth* canal.

It's true that some mothers, nearing delivery and shortly afterwards, feel sad, missing their pregnancies. Though some women do suffer hormonal difficulties, this is not so much a natural response to giving birth as a cultural effect. Pregnant women in the abstract are taken for madonnas, while women who are not pregnant are read for whores. With those models for choices, who *wouldn't* be sorry to see a pregnancy end? And given the equally artificial choice between heaven and hell, who wouldn't rather go to heaven?[9] The problem is that those choices—*any either/or* choices—*are* artificial. This is why an *either/or*, black-and-white world view has to be maintained by force.

The perspectives overwhelmed by the idea that spirit and matter are separate were not all charmingly pastoral, of course. But even those that incorporated more blood and gore than Wicca does[10] are alike in forming around a premise of reincarnation, which implies that spirit and matter are *not* separate, at least not entirely. In every life there is some "karma" to be worked out, and this is taken for granted in most Pagan religions. By contrast, most monotheistic systems give you just the one chance, and after that, you're in for eternal reward or eternal punishment.

And so it does come back to the issue of consciousness. Eternal reward or punishment disallows us a chance to learn from our mistakes or to build upon our successes. Self-consciousness is a prerequisite to learning from mistakes and letting good ideas grow, and so is a relatively broad understanding of the world. Wicca cel-

---

[9] I'm told that Mark Twain argued for going to hell because all his friends would be there, and in the South there's a wonderful expression: *Heaven for climate, Hell for company.* But generally speaking . . . .

[10] Hinduism, for instance, and various Polynesian and Central and South American traditions.

ebrates this consciousness, this knowing, this cultivation and harvest and feasting on fruit still forbidden to some.

Mortal life is a valuable experience—else, why would mortal life continue when matter could revert to energy and never compose itself again? Mortal life is *pleasing* to the God and Goddess (who declares in Her Charge that "all acts of love and pleasure are My rituals"). By living it we both celebrate Them and offer to Them. All of our sensations and sensibilities become part of what Jung called the collective unconscious[11] and so enrich the whole of the universe, life and all, every time we die, like a rich forest humus.

Wicca does not find us *guilty* of being human, and our Goddess charges us to enjoy ourselves: "sing, feast, dance, make music and love," She tells us. "Nor do I ask aught of sacrifice," She goes on. "I have been with you always," and "behold, I am the Mother of all things, and My love is poured forth across the Lands."

That I know of, there is no Wiccan liturgical material directing us to fear death, which is but a reunion with the Gods and our ancestors. "On Earth," the Goddess says to us in Her Charge, "I give knowledge of the Spirit Eternal, and beyond death, I give peace, and freedom, and reunion with those who have gone before." So we are not loath to sing and dance and feast—and yes, even make jokes—about death. It does not mean we feel our losses less deeply.

We *do* feel grief deeply, and one reason is that we do not hide our feelings from one another. As in many diving endeavors, you can go deeper into your emotions with a buddy. In what 'dancer

---

[11]A decent source for things Jungian is *The Portable Jung*, translated by R.F.C. Hull and edited by Joseph Campbell, published by Penguin Books in New York in 1976. Jung defines the collective unconscious as "a part of the psyche which can [be] . . . distinguished from a personal unconscious by the fact that it does not, like the latter, owe its existence to personal experience, and consequently is not a personal acquisition. [T]he contents of the collective unconscious owe their existence exclusively to heredity. Whereas the personal unconscious consists for the most part of *complexes*, the content of the collective unconscious is made up essentially of *archetypes*."

and I call our "extended coven," the several Witches of various Traditions who share social and religious life with each other here, we know a lot of each other's business, and share each other's feelings, hopes, dreams, fears, and the personal pilgrimages upon which somebody's always embarking.

Because we share an ideal of perfect love and perfect trust, which we do *not* think impossible to attain in our lives here and now, we tend to be very open with one another. If any one of us does something stupid or hurtful, the whole community becomes aware of it very quickly. More important, perhaps, the whole community responds (or at least tries to) *supportively*.

There is a presumption that "mistakes" are innocent even when we are angered by them. Thus, if someone in our community behaves offensively, we want to know what's the matter and how we can help, rather than getting mad *or* even. We have seen situations that had the potential to be personally devastating and destructive to the whole community resolved peaceably and with creativity and growth, because we have chosen to take cooperative rather than combative attitudes.[12]

And how can we do this? We live in an aggressive, competitive, zero-sum[13] culture, and beyond that, we may have to deal with personal criticism and attacks against which we might feel entitled to rail. Yet we do not abandon our fundamental love and trust, and we are not deterred from treating each other with respect.

We don't feel spiritually inadequate or defensive, so we can (though we're still learning how) acknowledge our real feelings. Knowing that our real feelings are acceptable to the God/dess, we can even laugh at ourselves. And because Wicca calls mirth a sacrament, we can laugh at death, too, without dishonor.

---

[12]Check out Starhawk's *Truth or Dare: Encounters with Power, Authority and Mystery*, published by Harper & Row in San Francisco in 1987. And also see M. Scott Peck's books.

[13]Lester Thurow's coinage. He's an economist who proposes that the economy should balance out exactly: if I have lots, you must settle for little.

Death is inevitable. So is Life: this is our belief. Furthermore, life and death, even on the mundane planes, are inextricable. Life feeds on life. We eat. We walk upon the earth. We drive cars. We move rocks. We burn wood. We slap mosquitoes. We all do countless things every day that might result in death for someone or something. The Goddess understands this: She learned it from Death Himself when She descended to confront Him.

But we all do countless things every day, wherever we are, that make continued life possible for other people and things, or that enhance other lives. There is a balance, and this is affirmed to us in every Sabbat. Our coven camps over several Sabbats a year, and the intimate, intricate relationship between life and death is quite clear out in the woods.

One Litha (the mid-summer Sabbat) the point was made—pretty pointedly, too—when we witnessed the death of a nest of three big-mouthed baby birds. It was sad, and yet, camping by a river that weekend under the relentless southwestern Midsummer Sun, it was hard not to surrender to joy as well. The Farrars[14] said that "at Midsummer, the 'process' aspect is reflected in the other God-theme—that of the Oak King and Holly King. At Midsummer, the Oak King, God of the Waxing Year, falls to the Holly King, his twin, the God of the Waning Year, *because the blazing peak of summer is also, by its very nature, the beginning of the Holly King's reign, with its inexorable progression to the dark nadir of midwinter*, when he in turn will die at the hands of the reborn Oak King." [Emphasis mine.] Perhaps those baby birds represented "the Oak King's midsummer death."

The Farrars also remind us that the Goddess never dies, but only presents us with different aspects; at Midsummer, "she shows her Death-in-Life aspect; her Earth-body is exuberantly fecund and sensuous . . . yet she knows it is a transient zenith, and at the same times she presides over . . . death." We did enjoy the

---

[14]Janet and Stewart Farrar, *A Witches Bible Compleat, Combined Volumes I and II* (Magickal Childe, New York, 1984). The section about Midsummer starts on page 93.

Summer's height on that trip: riverbank grasses reaching nearly to our shoulders, supple, green-leaved young trees enfolding us at every step, the cold, noisy water glittering with gold-rich sand and pebbles, warm breezes. But not without a price, not ever without a price. We just have to remember that life is a tool, and one doesn't haggle over the price.

But this price—is it punishment, Nature's way of accusing us? As a Wiccan, I say it is not. Is it punishment that we must exhale every breath we take in? Modern Wiccan thealogy[15] doesn't explain anything in terms of divine wrath, but sees exchanges of energy. Breath and other of the body's functions are particularly physical workings of the basic magic. Wiccans understand life, the universe, and everything as a "spiral dance," and understand further that this is the structure of nature.[16] It would be as reasonable to say that having *bones* is punishment, when skeletons are our natural physical framework.

Because Wicca doesn't hold the cyclical nature of life to be less than ideal, Wiccans don't have to think of death as punishment. While the death of those baby birds was not part of our plan, their deaths were still "in the service of life." We may be inclined to say, *Awwwwww*, but we know, really, that without anything dying, nothing could be reborn.

Change is, in fact, what keeps the sacred spiral turning. It is one of the physical forms Longing takes. Were there no change—since all change is a manifestation of death and rebirth—there could be no growth, no celebration. Life would be lifeless without change, and to judge *change* by a standard of *stasis* is at the very least coun-

---

[15] In *The Spiral Dance*, Starhawk credits religious scholar Naomi Goldenburg with coining this word from *thea*, the Greek work for *goddess*.

[16] This understanding is supported by 1992's revelations that the universe *is*, and virtually always *was* structured. As reported in the *Arizona Daily Star* on April 24, 1992, that structure was detected in faint left-over hot spots—radiation footprints—left by the expanding universe when it was but 300,000 years old. Lawrence Berkeley Lab astrophysicist George Smoot was quoted as saying about this evidence of structure that "if you're religious, it's like looking at God." Or Goddess.

terintuitive. Wicca's an intuitive and experiential religion, which makes it appropriate to see change as both fundamental and desirable. If you're looking to learn from experience, it's helpful to have more of it rather than less.

Of course, when I say "learn from our experience," I don't mean just our own personal experience in this life. No, and I mean not only the experiences of all the lives we can personally remember. We learn also from the experiences of our families and friends, our cultures and ethnic groups, and the experience of our species as well. We can even learn from the experience of other species in all the kingdoms and dimensions.

That we *do* learn and grow by trial and error doesn't mean that after making one mistake we'll never make others of the same kind. It is not characteristic of Wiccan thought to isolate incidents and judge them by any absolute standard. Rather, it is characteristic of Wiccan thought to recognize that life and death are not opposites but complements. Nothing and nobody ever really dies. The mountain may be gone, but you can dig your toes into the beach it becomes.

It is the nature of Individuality to be mortal; it is the nature of mortality to experience death. The experience of death is what makes a life individual. It is not a punishment, it is not a pitfall. We are sad to see the forms pass, but as the chant assures us, "the Circle of Life remains." We all come, after all, from the Goddess, and to Her we shall return. We and the cut flowers on our altars and every drop of rain and all the baby birds that were and are and evermore shall be, return to Her. And because She is both eternal *and* generative, we are also all reborn.

In a paper that a friend of mine, Rev. Christine Dungan, wrote[17] for a religious studies course several years ago, we are reminded that "There are three areas of support critical to the dying person: med-

---

[17]Christine K. Dungan, *The Impact of Varied Religious Traditions on the Approach of Clergy to Death and Dying: Four Personal Reflections* (1985) (unpublished).

ical, emotional and spiritual. The first is addressed most appropriately by hospital staff and physicians and the second by family and friends. But for spiritual help, the dying patient will most often turn to clergy." Among the Wiccan community, that can be any of us.

Something that Wiccan clergy will have noticed is that for the most part, there are no colleges or even classes regularly or conveniently available where we can get the training we need to be good counselors to the dying. We can, and I believe we should, watch for classes offered at local hospitals or clinics, junior or four-year colleges, and other extension services. There are a number of books in stores and libraries from which we can learn about the physical processes of dying, but this is one of too few specifically *religious* materials for *Wiccan* clergy on the subject of death.

In Dungan's paper, it becomes clear that Catholic, Protestant, and Jewish clergy can rely on common scripture and on generally accepted doctrine (although the degree to which individual clerics depend on that material varies greatly according to denomination and even where in the country the congregation is settled). Wicca has no universal formal scripture and no (or almost no) dogma.

There is the Rede, there is the Three-fold Law, and there is the Charge of the Goddess (which does vary among Traditions, expressing much the same perspective in many very beautiful ways). A Wiccan priest/ess's orientation to death is influenced by the teachings of the religion in which s/he was raised, too. A roomful of priest/esses might well agree on many thealogical points, but our individual emphases will vary.

When a Christian or Jewish minister or rabbi counsels a dying congregant, the dying man or woman expects to hear "facts" and be reassured—s/he expects set points of belief to be reiterated, maybe clarified. When a Wiccan priest/ess counsels someone on the subject of death, we can reiterate a belief in reincarnation and in the Goddess's unconditional love and the God's graceful and protective guidance through the process.

There is no hell for Wiccans to avoid or escape, of course, and neither is there any formally standardized dogma or official images to quote or conjure. What Wiccan clergy do for the dying is guide their meditations and encourage the dying covener (or solitary, or cowan!) to draw upon her own experience, his own intuition.

We must remember how the Goddess charges us: "For if that which you seek you do not find within, you shall surely never find it without." Our Wiccan faith is as convinced that we will find what we seek within as it is confident of our description of the realms beyond death. In truth, that which we find within is *all* we will be able to find without.

This is a tricky concept, slippery on good days, and it can be hard to hold onto in moments of crisis, especially in a culture that denies it both subtly and grossly. Weakened by physical disease, discouraged by a non-Pagan family's ignorance of or opposition to Wicca, troubled by financial obligations, concerned about projects that might be left unfinished, and working through grief, a dying Witch may need a priest/ess's active guidance. But the patient's reassurances must, ultimately, be her own convictions, his own discovery *within* of what s/he needs.

While clergy of most religions understand death as an external circumstance to which we are inevitably vulnerable, Wiccans understand death also to be an extension of inner exploration. Death restores us to the Goddess's Wholeness, which is the ultimate and universal cosmic "inner." She has, after all, been with us from the beginning. For Wiccans, it's birth, not death, that takes us to the "outer." Many of us believe that in the Summerland, we are counseled by mentoring spirits who help us prepare for rebirth, which process mirrors death in many ways.

If Wiccan clergy haven't any universal scriptures or dogma to quote, we do have the experience of Initiation on which to call, and that is something deeply meaningful and symbolic to everyone who's been through it. I remember thinking when our son was born that the physical sensations I noticed could just as well be preceding my own death as the Explorer's birth. (I don't mean the pain, for that was ever-so-clearly to do with birth. I mean the *other* physical sensations, the sounds, the way a peculiar tingle crept through me, and the feeling, half-physical and half-intuitive, that under just a little more stress I could have left my body, right through all my pores, pulled myself together, and moved on.) Giving birth and being born are both *very* initiatory experiences, and so is death; and they are all intricately related, not really separate as they appear to modern Western culture.

The mirror we hold up when an Initiate's blindfold is removed is—and is meant to be—an aspect of the *light* toward which we are drawn at death. The point is that with all our imperfections (which are purified, if not corrected, when we face them and resolve to work on them) we are God/dess.

To Christians, Jesus said *he* was the way and the light, and many Christians take that to mean that they should be as much like Jesus as possible, in order to be as pleasing to God as possible. "The soul has to be as perfect as possible," the Catholic priest told Dungan in his interview, "because God is perfect."

Wiccans believe in perfection, too: perfect love and perfect trust are among many Traditions' initiatory passwords. But this perfection describes relationships, not the people in them. Each of us is responsible for what we contribute to all of our relationships; there's nobody else any of us is supposed to be like. We are *each* and *all* "the way" and "the light," and we achieve reunion by becoming as fully *ourselves* as possible. Many Wiccans take the Faery tradition's advice (quoted by Starhawk) to "follow the self to find the Self."

Because Wiccans do believe in reincarnation, Wiccan priest/esses don't talk about heaven and hell, but about the Goddess's promise of peace, freedom, and reunion beyond death. Unlike the Catholics, Wiccans don't believe that we ever "gain an everlasting dwelling place in Heaven," as Father Smith told Dungan.

Most religions teach that there is a . . . well, "paradise" is a Persian word, "heaven" derives from Anglo-Saxon, and many neo-Pagans say "Summerland." It is an experience, a perspective—not a place of physical coordinates. We talk about the Summerland as if it were a physical place, though, because we are physical creatures. Incarnate, we require a place, a material context, in which to exist. It is as natural to use physical metaphors for the Summerland as it is to use organic metaphors for deity.

In those metaphors we describe the Summerland's sunny shores and we identify it with the dark Underworld as well. We place it on the astral and we call it an aspect of the Goddess's womb. In my coven's Tradition, the Summerland is a microcosm of the Whole, a confluence of all the realms and dimensions. The Summerland is a way-station between the Poles, the space and time between the Whole and Individuality. The Summerland is where we are transformed, whether we're "coming" or "going." Our eternity is not static, nor is it judgmental. In the Summerland, we look forward to reintegration, not retribution.

There is no eternal Heaven or Hell in the God/dess, just r/evolving circuits 'round the Wheel, death and rebirth being essentially the same experience. We go . . . West when we die; "over the Western Sea" is one way we say it. West is the direction of the sunset, release into the otherworld of Night, the grave, the womb. We go West, as adventurers have always gone.

Something else that many monotheisms affirm is that, as Father Smith put it, "Human nature is always afraid of the unknown." I do not find that to be true. I think it is human nature to be *excited* by the unknown. Many of us have been conditioned to interpret that excitement as anxiety and fear; but I do not believe that we are naturally inclined to fear the unknown. I think we are naturally inclined through curiosity to explore the unknown. (Otherwise, we wouldn't have had pioneers or astronauts.) Wicca draws on ancestral examples that teach us to approach the unknown in a spirit of adventure rather than fearfully.

Our own mortality is difficult to accept. This isn't necessarily because we are afraid to die but simply because from the incarnate perspective it is almost impossible to imagine—to image or model—being unincarnate. Sooner or later, because we're working with three-dimensional brains, we come back to three-dimensional imagery.

In meditation and ritual, we sometimes "flash" into under-standings that transcend the physical matrix on which the mater-ial plane depends. We can do this well enough and often enough to be convinced that life does exist in nonmaterial forms, and that the universe follows rules on those other planes roughly parallel to the ones we live by here. Yet while we are incarnate, we are under some constraints in the way our brains can formulate concepts, and that limitation of incarnation is one we have to accept along with mortality.

But in Wiccan philosophy, mortality is not a finite condition, either. It's a state into which our energies can, and do, enter more than once, just as a light bulb can be turned on and off. Wiccans don't expect to be incarnate only once, any more than most of us expect to enter a room in our house only one time and then never again.

That gives us a very different understanding of death than soci-ety's stereotype. We can concentrate on learning from our mis-takes rather than worrying about not making any. We have a chance to pick up where we left off (ideally) and learn even more from our next incarnation, and from previous incarnations if we have remembered or deduced anything about them, rather than having just the one chance like an entrant in an athletic meet who completes his event and then waits to see if anyone does better.

We do not compare ourselves to any Perfect Being, but trust that within each of us the perfection of any given incarnation is latent, and that ultimately our incarnate experiences will enhance the Whole. Our concern with perfection is this: that in every life that we know ourselves to be Witches, we work in and toward perfect love and perfect trust, for that is one of the signs by which we know death to be perfectly safe.

Unique individual experiences change the experience of Wholeness, thus allowing it to reinspire new Individual experiences, in turn re-inspiring the Whole. That is the rhythm of the spiral dance. Our various mortal experiences do enlarge and enhance the Wholeness to which we return between incarnations.

One of the ways that Wicca is different from dominant Western religious traditions is that it is initiatory. Wiccan Initiations generally involve a symbolic death and rebirth. Most teachers insist that their apprentices face their "inner Guardians," those secret fears to which we give such enormous power by hiding them in shame and guilt.

The reason that apprentices are asked to admit these secrets is that admitting them confronts, and in that confrontation (conducted in the safety of ritual) the fears back down. The power fear once held *over* the Initiate is reintegrated, becoming part of the Initiate's own power. In Wicca, this inner power—some people call it strength of character or inner peace—is understood as power *with* the natural world, as realized kinship to the rest of life.

A discovery that delights all Initiates is that the "death" of the ego, the suspension of our awareness of individuality, results *not* in oblivion or exploitation but in a magnificent sense of enlargement, of expanded consciousness and *belonging* to the Whole universe. In an Initiation rite a Wiccan "dies" to her old life and all its insecurities, and is "reborn" to a greater understanding of natural relationships. Witches have an expectation that physical death results in rebirth, too, and in Initiation, we have a model through which to understand it nonthreateningly. We also have the assurance that the death of our body is the "lesser" death.

Part of what we do while we're living any given life is explore the interpretive landscape of mortality. If we didn't work with our experience and potential the way sculptors work with their clay, then we would not be making original contributions. It is no disadvantage to be without dogma! It is a freedom, an affirmation and validation of our Individual experience, mistakes and all.

Like ministers and priests of any denomination, Wiccan clergy need to be very clear about our feelings and philosophies toward these issues in order to be effective counselors at death. Understanding the basic tenets of Wiccan thealogy, even though much of it is subjective, is the foundation for the creativity we need to bring to the sociocultural process of dying.

Especially because Wicca is still poorly understood by many mainstream professionals, the tension between the way a Wiccan priest/ess or patient might wish to proceed and what a doctor or hospital staff might wish to do can be very high. Because our social institutions—including medical facilities—tend to be organized hierarchically and with some *either/or, right/wrong* presumptions at bottom, it's easy to be intimidated and drawn into mundane confrontation.

So that we do not unwittingly violate the Rede as we priest/ess anyone through death, Wiccan clergy need to recognize this tension as *energy*, and need to develop ways of directing that energy appropriately.

Because there are temporal and legal needs to meet when someone dies, it's important that Wiccan priest/esses give the whole process of and attitude toward death their consideration *before* they need to deal with it, or before it has to be dealt with *again*. (Off-putting as a bad death or funeral experience can be, it's instructive.)

While Wiccan priest/esses can read each other's books almost endlessly, and learn much from them, it is also important that they communicate meaningfully with their own communities. Here we've held workshops about death. How well organized such workshops will be wherever they're held will depend, of course, on the experience of the community. But even if you spend an hour or so deciding what you want to talk about, how you want to approach the subject—even if several people ramble rather widely or seem to skirt the subject in the first meeting—communication will be opened and appreciated.

If you make it possible for people to meet whenever a concern is raised by any experience—maybe something somebody read or heard about rather than anything that happened directly to someone in your circle or network—the issues will begin to define themselves.

Giving each other safe times and spaces to talk, to cry, to remember, to preface what they say with, "this might sound stupid, but . . ." is of critical importance. It's also an aspect of the counseling Wiccan priest/esses can offer each other and the community. Holding these workshops on new or full Moons will affirm the holy nature of your feelings about death, and the sanctity of your right to share them.

In ten years, things will be different. We can't—and don't want to—stop change. But it *is* our "thing" to *direct* change; and that means we can influence the "different" it will be in ten years. Oh, we'll still be mortal, and more of us, as the huge 'boomer generation ages, will be thinking about death. Something we can do for our own future and for those who will follow us into middle age and elderhood is begin *now* to talk openly about death, about our feelings, our ideas, our hopes and ideals in terms of alternatives to the dreaded tubes and wires, alternatives to today's social and religious attitudes.

I believe that when we undertake that clerical duty, we will find great reward, not only personally and not only in the improved understanding of Wicca our work can give the public, but in the health of the planet generally. Death has been closeted just as Witches have been. I believe that Wicca's understanding of death has much to offer, not only to people who find their own present understanding of death frightening or inadequate, but to our outlook on *life* as well.

Thealogy

Wicca teaches that life is sacred and wonderful and fundamentally good. Wicca holds that everything—every life, every landscape, every system, every soul—is interrelated. Wicca accepts the laws of physics and the power of love.

Wicca is the descendant of ancient, affirmative nature religions, from the caves where Trois Frères' antlered priests are painted, and from the cultures that carved the Venuses of Willendorf. Given its modern form and Anglo-Saxon name by Gerald Gardner in the mid-twentieth century, Wicca carries on many ancestral traditions and beliefs.

One of these, shared by all Paganisms I can think of, is that the world of spirit and symbol is as matter-of-fact and significant as the physical world. Wiccans believe the Goddess and the God exist in both Worlds,[1] as active forces in the physical realm and as the Mother Goddess and Her Horned Lover and Son in spirit.

Goddess is all that is eternal and generative. As the female produces seeds and gives birth in the plant and animal worlds, so the generative principle is female in Wiccan thealogy. God is the name we give to the mortal cycle, all that dies and is reborn. Wiccans believe that mortal forms—including our own—come from the

---

[1] Saying "both worlds" is a convenience, a figure of speech. Many of us use it when we cast our Circles, which we conjure to be a boundary between the "world of men" and "the realms of the Mighty Ones." The astral realm is wide and varied and many religions distinguish its regions as several worlds, even as just about everybody distinguishes *this* region of it as a clearly defined world.

The Charge of the Goddess

Campsight Coven's version, based on
Doreen Valiente's original

I

Whenever you have need of anything, once in the month
(and better it be when the Moon is full)
then you shall assemble in some sacred place,
there to adore My spirit, who am Queen of all the Witches.
There you shall be free from slavery
and in token that you are truly free, you shall be naked in your rites.
Sing! Feast! Dance! Make music and love, all in My presence,
for Mine is the spirit of ecstasy; and Mine as well is joy on Earth.
Mine is the Cup of the Wine of Life: the Cauldron of Cerridwen,
that is the holy Grail of Immortality.
On Earth, I give knowledge of the spirit eternal; and beyond death,
I give peace, and freedom, and reunion with those who have gone before.
Nor do I ask aught of sacrifice, for behold! I am the Mother of all things,
and My love is poured forth across the Lands.

II

I, who am the beauty of the green Earth and the white Moon among the stars,
the mystery of the Ocean, and the desire in all Hearts,
I call upon your souls to arise, and come unto Me—
for I am the soul of Nature that gives life to the Universe.
From Me all things proceed, and unto Me all things return.
Let My worship be in the heart that rejoices, for behold,
all acts of love and pleasure are my rituals.
Let there be beauty and strength, power and compassion, honor and humility,
and mirth and reverence with you;
and you who would seek to know Me, know this:
that all your seeking and yearning shall be to no avail,
unless you know the mystery:
if that which you seek you do not find within, you shall surely never find it without.
For behold:
I have been with you from the beginning,
and I am That Which is Attained at the end of all desire.

eternal, and that it is through our mortality that the eternal is revealed.

One cannot create or destroy energy, after all. One can only transform it to matter of almost infinite variety. So Wiccans believe in transformation, including that kind of transformation we call reincarnation. After a rest in the Summerland, the dead return in new bodies, to rejoin their clans in other generations. Open your mind to the idea that *all* of life—beings and the environments in which they have evolved and grown up—is a Whole, a system not unlike this planet's oceans and atmosphere, with complexities and consequences and correlations.[2]

Understand this Whole in terms of its systems, and the idea that death is a permanent separation makes no sense. There's no place, no condition, that isn't part of the process, the cycles. There is no experience—not birth, not death, and nothing in between—that is not a microcosmic expression of the Whole process, at the same time that it is an Individual element of the process. The process is that of dying (becoming Whole) and being reborn (becoming Individual).

"Mine is the secret of the Door that opens upon youth," the Goddess tells us in the Farrars' version of Her Charge. The "secret" is Her perspective, which is Wholeness; death is a door to the Whole, just as birth is a door to Individuality. To be reborn from Wholeness we must first rejoin the Whole, and this we do by dying.

Death is said to have occurred when measurable bodily functions can no longer be measured: when the heart and breathing stop, when there are no more brain waves. Depending on the circumstances of death, the body may look quite different than it did when someone was living in it. According to many Eastern traditions, the process of death, the "moment of death," as we West-

[2]Oberon Zell developed what's now well known as "The Gaia Hypothesis" in 1970. Dr. James Lovelock, who has most of the publishing fame on the topic, didn't get onto it until 1972. See *Green Egg*, vol. XXI, no. 81 (Beltane, 1988).

erners call it, is a noisy and sensational experience for the one dying. Vitality withdraws from the feet toward the crown: the body gets cold from the feet upward, and the dying lose feeling in the extremities as consciousness focuses in the head.

In control of the process—aware of what to expect and practiced in techniques to direct the energy—a person's death can be accomplished in about 20 minutes. It may not take even that long to achieve the physical state medical equipment can identify as death, or it may take much longer if there's a lot of interference. Whether this physical death completes or is the whole of the death experience is another question. Many teachers of Wicca describe us as having more than one body. In addition to the physical, we have an astral or etheric body, and one or more additional psycho-energetic bodies,[3] which disperse at different rates.

A preponderance of evidence shows that there is one experience we are *all* likely to have at death. It is an experience of swift movement toward a bright light which welcomes us to another sort of existence. Although soaring toward the light is recalled as unpleasant by some who have been drawn back to their erstwhile incarnation, most report that when a welcome is extended, fear, doubt, and stress cease to be meaningful.

Some medicos observe that these near-death experiences are hallucinatory products of an oxygen-deprived brain as if that observation invalidates the experience. If you break your leg, the pain is the bio-chemical expression of a mechanical problem, but that doesn't mean it isn't real and doesn't make a difference; bet you're still gonna want a pain pill. Subjective doesn't mean invalid. There's no need to discount the products of brain chemistry; everything anybody does is the product of brain chemistry, after all. What Wicca calls us to do is to come to terms, subjectively,

---

[3] I think a very nice primer on this sort of thing is Diane Stein's *Stroking the Python: Women's Psychic Lives* (Llewellyn Publications, St. Paul, 1988). Chapter 2 discusses "auras, chakras and psychic bodies."

with the idea of death as a station on the circuit rather than some final destination.[4]

Furthermore, our Traditions' liturgical material supports our inner questing, and there is no Wiccan dogma to substitute for personal experience; no dogma could express it. The *experience* of death as a gateway, a twin of birth, is so much at the core of Wicca that it is both why and how Wicca is an initiatory religion.

Wiccans generally believe that everything we know or can imagine is part of nature, and nature is cyclical—the Moon's phases and the Seasons; birth, growth, death, and rebirth. We believe the polarities we see in these cycles are complementary, not adversarial. We do not see the aspects of the world as being inevitably in conflict.

We believe in magic as a natural force. Just as gravity keeps our feet firmly planted on the physical surface of our rotating Earth, so magic bonds us on the psycho-spiritual plane to every other creature and feature that shares the planet with us. Working magic takes different skills than working gravity, but the magic Wiccans do is no more sinister or supernatural than ballroom dancing!

Witches believe that the Threefold Law holds true in all the worlds, and experience confirms that what we put into life is what we'll get back from it. The Wiccan Rede ("rede" is Anglo-Saxon for counsel or advice) is "An ye harm none, do as ye will." We believe in the wisdom and practicality, both spiritually and materially, of the Rede and the Law.

Now, we've all heard, "You made your own bed, now lay in it," and we've all heard crude misinterpretations of "karma," holding that whatever lousy stuff happens to you in this life, you either "chose" or "deserved." This interpretation is not consistent with what I understand of Wiccan philosophy, and I want to take a moment to discuss it, because it's important to a lot of us.

Ideas about the way things that happen in this life influence

[4]Despite William Gray's diatribe against our calling ourselves Witches in his text and in a dedicated appendix, his Rollright Ritual is a hair-raisingly neat summary of the process. My copy is *By Standing Stone & Elder Tree* from Llewellyn (1990).

things that happen in the next have stimulated religious philosophy for as long as the human race can remember. A common Western understanding is that if you're bad in this life, you'll suffer for it in the next. Many people take that to mean that if, for instance, you abuse somebody now, you'll get, or you got, abused in another life; and it can definitely work like that through the material plane's generations.

But must someone who leads a cruel life return to feel the misery s/he once caused? What goes around comes around, we say; and you get out of life what you put into it. What you give to the world returns to you threefold, the Wiccan Three-fold Law has reminded us for generations. The Shirley MacLaine school says it means you have to keep coming back till you get it right. This is a pretty authoritarian idea, very useful to wielders of power-over. I don't think Wiccans are under any obligation to accept it.

What seems to me consistent with the Wiccan world view is the notion that we are born, and we reincarnate, to have as wide an experience of Individuality as possible. It seems to me reasonable to think that we are social and empathetic and sympathetic by nature—multidimensional—so that we can be enlarged and enriched in many ways, precisely because there is no one-and-only legitimate perspective.

This suggests to me that we don't have to literally endure a physical experience before we can appreciate it at all, so reincarnation needn't be "pay-back." I find no support in Wiccan liturgy for an interpretation of reincarnation as either punitive or rewarding. To the contrary, the Goddess demands naught of sacrifice, and beyond death, She gives peace, and freedom, and reunion with those who have gone before. I read all of this to mean that you get to keep coming back till you get it all. ("All," of course, keeps getting bigger as the experiences of more and more lives add to it.)

There is much evidence to support the idea that consciousness survives the death of the body. The evidence is universal, spanning epochs and cultures and all the seas. It is mystical and mundane.

One way to understand this idea is in pottery's terms. You are dying, an unglazed pot shard, and your transition through the tunnel of light is a kiln of sorts; your attitudes as you leave your body are the glaze. Different thoughts and approaches will give you different colors and textures as death burns away the broken bits and trimmings and restores you to the *whole* clay pot, the Cauldron, the Mother.

Feelings or thoughts of fear, greed, self-doubt, anger, bitterness, etc. are going to glaze you in your worst colors; the depth of those feelings will determine how deeply their glaze penetrates you. The most ancient records of human wisdom absolutely presume that your feelings at death color your next life. The advice of these ancient teachings is to confront your own mortality before you face it physically, so that you have rehearsed the proper response to the end of your present incarnation.

Wiccans generally do not believe that the Goddess and God play figures or dolls with our lives. That is, there's no Big Lady in the Sky going, "Okay, now you say this and he says this and then the building falls on you and you're dead, ahahahahaha." No pre-destination in that sense, either. Neither do we believe that any of us lay back in the Summerland's lounge chairs working from a checklist of horrible things we think it'd be fun to have happen to us next time around. "Yes, I think I'll have both legs blown off in battle," or "It'd be a nice touch if my child were wiped out by a drunken driver," is not how it works.

What I believe is this: from the Summerland, we make some very basic choices, equivalent to saying at the start of a vacation, "Let's drive east and take the interesting turns." You can't know exactly what you'll encounter, and even if one of your encounters is with a serial killer or a pothole that rips your tire to shreds, nobody'd be likely to say that's what you *wanted* to have happen. No, you just looked at the map and saw all those blue highways out there and thought this one might be an interesting direction to try.

So it is with the lives we "choose." Having been around before doesn't make us omniscient. Most of us don't remember past lives, and aren't real sure what our calling is in this one. Our unresolved death traumas from past lives are usually not active in our conscious minds, so the ways in which they influence us cannot be called conscious choices. (In fact, "choice" is a sort of misleading word, because what I really mean here is that we tend to come back to lives that will give us opportunities to resolve whatever's unfinished from past experiences. We gravitate back to lives that can give us relevant experience more than we "choose" our incarnations like cruise vacations.)

So the things that happen to us in this life, "good" or "bad," are not choices like things you order from a catalogue are choices. They are consequences, in the way cancer may follow from too much second-hand smoke. We don't choose or control all the details that give our lives their unique cachet, but we can usually be held responsible for our reactions to the things that happen in our lives. We're not always in control of what happens to us, but we can learn to stay in control of our responses, our attitudes. Of course, by "staying in control" I don't mean "suppressing our feelings." The whole point is that you can't control anything unless you start from freedom; and if you're shackled by fear or imprisoned by ignorance, you're not free.

The Wiccan ideal as I understand it is to be aware of your feelings, understand and accept their energies, and then reshape those energies according to your will—and that process is guided, ideally, by love. (And that's not love as Hallmark defines it; that's love as Starhawk defines it. It's the force that holds the universe together, which includes romantic love *and* "molecular love" and everything in between.)

You can't keep "bad" things from happening to you or people you care about. You can be careful and plan ahead, and that will smooth things out some, but none of us is in complete and detailed charge of the world. Life is a colonial organism and we are not its only cells. All you can do, sometimes, is remember that doors don't close without other ones opening, that there is something to learn from everything. Every specific experience enlarges your experience as a whole, and every individual's experience(s) enlarges life as a whole—thus adding to what individuals can experience.

That beyond death She offers peace and freedom, and that She asks naught of sacrifice are strong indications that S/he does not punish. Her love is unconditional. But ... but ... no punishment? What if the dead guy was a real villain? Well, villains die, like the God and everybody else. That's all that needs to happen. The God/dess is not vengeful or punishing. The Goddess is the Mother of all things and Her love is poured forth across the Lands, and there are no conditions set upon Her love. So, no, there is no punishment, not in the commonly accepted sense of the word, not even for villains.

However, the process of dying can be called a process of facing the Guardians, facing the reality of your life, facing your fears and guilts.[5] This can be an arduous process, frightening to people who expect harsh judgment. For such people, the ordinary effects of bodily death may be terrifying. Someone who expects to be punished in the afterlife will find punishment. Quaking or defiant, the fear and acceptance of punishment, and the denial of immanent joy that fear represents, *are* the punishment. It is self-imposed, a post-mortem act of will. Wicca's thealogy supports facing death without fear.

I want to get close enough to the energy to be charged with it, for then, because "I am Goddess," I can *change* that energy. It isn't usually easy, and it's almost never instantaneous: my best record is three days for changing some really unpleasant sort of knee-jerk

---

[5] Wicca doesn't support the concept of sin, and emphasizes responsibility more than guilt; but while we do not accept that being human is intrinsically guilty, we do know that people can be guilty of doing harm in the world. Intent matters, though: willful harm produces guilt along with responsibility, inadvertent harm produces, morally, only responsibility.

emotional responses into mostly more constructive energy; in other instances, it's taken years and years.

I don't think there's anything intrinsically wrong, either, in taking some issues with you from this life into others. I think it's pretty much a natural consequence of the effort/ability to keep large bits of ourselves together. We always lug some "baggage" around with us, and it's not all bad; some of it's souvenirs!

If you look at your own life, you'll see themes that you can trace from childhood, interests that you can't explain. These are inarticulate memories, some suggest, from past lives. Maybe so. Certainly when we say in our Initiations that ". . . you must return again at the same time and place as the loved one, and you must remember and love them again," we encourage each other to carry some "issues" from life to life. Why, even our family resemblances hint strongly that this is the natural way of things. I have found the aphorism "as above, so below" to be reliable so far, and it too suggests shared content.

The Anglo-Saxon cosmology which is part of Wicca's inheritance is symbolized by a "web of Wyrd," a semi-visual model of our interconnectedness.[6] What we can't control, we can interpret and, well, dance with. When we try to blame people for all their misfortunes, for getting their toes stepped on in the dance, you might say, we're forgetting that the world has more than one level, the web more than one strand; none of us is the only dancer.

The Web is only one analogy, too. There are other traditional ones—the World Tree, for instance—and more being developed. It's not terribly important what metaphors we use; it is terribly important that we learn that the world is more complex than we can measure, and we are more than islands of flesh and blood. Paraphrasing the Bard, there's more to heaven and earth than dreamt of in some philosophies.

---

[6]Brian Bates's doctoral thesis, *The Way of Wyrd*, published in 1983 by Century Publishing (and in 1984 by Book Club Associates) in London, is a great read on this subject.

Wicca does not divide "spirit and flesh," or make them irreconcilable by describing them as opposites. Life is not served by "opposition" as we commonly understand it. For Wiccans, spirit and flesh are mutual complements. The Whole (spirit) is incomplete without Individual experience, and the Individual (flesh) is incomplete without experiencing Wholeness. It is this complementary completion, this spiraling integration of individuality and wholeness we are always trying to achieve. It's the same thing science is trying to do in mathematical terms in the quest after a Unified Field Theory to integrate the four fundamental forces.

It is this call to balance that moves the universe. This calling is the beat of the spiral dance, a toe-tapping beat that just won't let us sit still at the side of the hall. Everything, everyone, everythought is compelled to respond to the beat, take its own steps in the dance.

Wiccans dance "the spiral dance" through the cycles of the planet and the cycles of our lives when we celebrate the eight Sabbats and thirteen Esbats that mark the Wheel of the Year. Sabbats are solar holidays that mark the Seasons; Esbats are observations of the Moon's phases. We think there's a lot to be learned from the [wholly sacred] natural world.

Now, we don't know just yet how many other planets are answering life's religious questions for people the way Mother Earth answers them for us. But if we *could* say with certainty that there are 42 of them or 6,542 of them, I would still say that She encompasses them as well, and that He is incarnate in whoever trips the mortal fantastic there. There is nothing science now knows, and I think nothing science can know, that contradicts Wiccan thealogy. There is nothing in Wiccan thealogy that requires us to ignore or deny anything science has learned about the worlds so far.

There are religions that would have us accept all that is generative and eternal as *male*. This contradicts our experience in the world, and so to maintain the contradictory assertion, our experience in the world must be discredited. Our experience of matter and spirit as fundamentally One, as an integrated Whole, was discredited by an enforced declaration that spirit and matter were not only *separate* but also inevitably in conflict. It was monotheistically mandated that life in the material realm, which used to set the standard for rightness and well-being, was poor, nasty, brutish and short, to borrow from Thomas Hobbes.[7]

No longer did most societies accept the authority and sanctity of the life force inherent in all the Mother's children and the planet. The premise that holiness is awarded or bestowed by a supernatural Source was formally enacted. Living with swords to their throats, people believed what they were told to believe, and in preserving the outward images of correct belief, they danced no longer.

Love survived, of course, but organized European Paganism did not, except in the human psyche. Through the Romantic Movement neo-Paganism re-emerged, and today's Wicca is an evocative reinterpretation of what was and might have been. A line in a popular chant goes, "We are the Witches, back from the dead." This rebirth took centuries, and is glorious, yet death still appears to some of us as punishment, spiritually as well as physically. This is a way that we are still kept from our full power.

It is true enough today that we assorted Pagans are still mostly poor, still in danger from public ignorance and fear. And it is still true that "they" can still overwhelm us with superior economic and political force. But it is, at least in Adventure Wicca's terms, only those who still fear death who are truly overcome.

Even knowing as we all do that this mortal experience won't last forever, a lot of people are still thinking that physical immortality was once a human privilege. One story is that immortality is

---

[7] The book was titled *Leviathan: or the matter, forme and power of a commonwealth ecclesiastical and civil,* and the edition we refer to was edited by Michael Oakeshott, published by Collier Books in New York in 1962.

now withdrawn to a spiritual province, to which our entrance can be denied for the smallest infractions. These infractions can be hard to avoid too, because they're defined differently in different times and places, sometimes by the same religion.

What Wiccans used to think was a historical legacy from the Dark Ages has been shown to be our lore.[8] The wonderful tales of secret midnight Sabbats in defiance of the Inquisition turn out to be legendary rather than literal. And there is no doubt that modern Wicca is very different from classical Witchcraft, too. However, because perception so influences reality, our modern perspective on Witchcraft has already built a strong faith that is enriched by, but not dependent on, historical lore. The thealogy we have recovered and revived and revised tells us that *there is no basis, in what we can accept as "fact" about the world, to fear or dread death.*

In *Deathing*, by Anya Foos-Graber,[9] material from the *Tibetan Book of the Dead* is presented in secular Western terms. This material, by her interpretation and others,[10] suggests that our several nonphysical bodies take a few days to disengage from the spent physical body, and the Individual's experience of reunion with the Whole is so overwhelming that the Individual may benefit from some coaching, as it were, through the (approximately) week-long process of death.

Through Cerridwen's Cauldron (Cerridwen is a mother goddess whose main symbol is the cauldron) the dead have always found restoration and rebirth. Most of us have heard of the "tunnel of light experience" reported by people whose bodies have been recovered from a state of clinical death. That experience is spoken

---

[8]Read Ronald Hutton's *The Triumph of the Moon* (Oxford University Press, 1999).

[9]Anya Foos-Graber, *Deathing, an Intelligent Alternative for the Final Moments of Life* (Nicholas-Hays, Inc., York Beach, Maine, 1989).

[10]Others include the Rev. Paul Beyerl, who has something to offer in his book *A Wiccan Bardo*; and Ly Warren-Clark in *The Way of the Goddess* offers some wonderful exercises in her Second Stage techniques; and though I do not know its text, I know the Rowan Tree Church's requiem is a seven-day rite.

of by mystics in many traditions. In Wicca's mythological inheritance, the details of that tunnel are described in terms of adventure and distraction: the Celtic heroes' journeys through Faerie or in magical archipelagos, the courtly French and British quests. The Hindu experience is described very differently in the *Book of the Dead*, which is less metaphorical than the surviving European texts.

But whether we are reminded by the medieval symbolism of the deeper significance of Sir Gawain's adventure with the Green Knight, for instance, or adopt the direct style of coaching offered in Eastern systems, we are trusting our lives to an understanding of reincarnation. "Life after life" is how Dr. Raymond Moody put it in the title of his 1975 book.[11]

---

[11]Raymond Moody, *Life After Life* (Bantam Books, New York, 1975).

Reincarnation

One way of describing what I think will happen is as a rollicking space adventure. I use this metaphor because we have a common cultural acceptance that space contains unimaginable sights and experiences, not because I really expect to find Tom Baker as Dr. Who in his TARDIS (or Jean-Luc on the *Enterprise*) behind the light. Whatever it is, though, I expect to experience it as wonderful, awesome, and totally attractive, definitely a no-regrets sort of thing.

More of us are better educated these days than ever before in recorded history, and we enjoy the freedom to work mundane magic (like political activism) as well as our traditional conjurations. We are beginning to see a "*hundredth monkey*"[1] or "critical mass" effect now, so that attitudes all over the world are changing, albeit slowly. These attitudes are superficially about rain forests and other threatened environments and the lives that depend on them, for we are finally noticing that ours are *among* the lives that depend on the health of the planet generally.

This coming so alarmingly clearly into focus for people now, folks are beginning to see it as a matter of their *own* life and death, both physically and spiritually. Our skill in directing this energy is one tool we can use to shape a life-friendly future, and a tool that

---

[1]Ken Keyes, Jr., *The Hundredth Monkey* (Vision Books, St. Mary, Kentucky, 1981). The idea is that when enough people (or monkeys) learn how to do a thing, by their own trials and errors or from each other, a sort of critical mass will be reached and suddenly just about everybody will mysteriously know how to do the same thing.

our ancestors through the generations used before us on smaller but equally intense and awesome cones of power.

Conventional religions, even Eastern ones, don't give us much support for these new attitudes, don't offer us, yet, many ways to channel the energy that these developing concerns raise. There are people who believe wholeheartedly that it's just fine to raze the planet entirely because their Savior is coming back and going to destroy everything as if with a ray-gun. There are many more folk who understand Armageddon to be metaphorical, maybe something like the change of attitude we, along with the planet, are going through right now.

There are people who don't really care what they leave to their children, whether there are parks or animals or wildernesses or blue skies or any Social Security benefits, because they believe that they're never coming back here, and that wherever they're going is the place that really matters. There are renters in my old neighborhood who act like that. They don't plan to stay long or come back, and they don't care if they're filling somebody *else's* alley with used plastic diapers and wrecked furniture. One of the problems with this attitude is that sometimes people end up staying places longer than they expected to, and then they have to deal with their own garbage anyhow. Better not to let it stack up, hmm?

Many Native American religions take into consideration the next seven generations to come. This isn't the same thing as Wiccans' belief in reincarnation, but it has a similar effect on the way we behave. Who with any power in a situation would choose to do something s/he knew would be harmful to her great[6th] grandchild, even if it were something that would profit her or her children or grandchildren? What Witch with power in a circumstance would willingly undertake a project that would muck up her future lives? Wiccans not only care about their great[6th] grandchildren, we consider the possibility that we might end up *being* one of our great[6th] grandchildren!

Eastern religions have been popular in the West since the 1960's, when they brought ideas and ways to express them to a "counterculture" that mourned, if inarticulately at times, the passing of humanity's ease in the natural world. Disconnected from our own cultural heritage, even in the thick of the Eurocentrism that has dominated the humanities and the sciences in the last couple of centuries, it is still not clear to everybody that ancient Anglo-European philosophies and cosmologies produced competent religions.

Dissociating from a hierarchical, patriarchal, judgmental system that seems to many to do more harm than good, many Western seekers of spiritual wisdom turned—and still turn—to Eastern philosophies. Yet the denouement in their stories is that it's all an external deity's dream. In the end, there is *still* a choice to be made between form and spirit.

Wicca does not think so. Obviously, at least to me, if *either* form *or* spirit were a vastly better state than the other, well, then, everything would attain that better state, there'd be no interest in returning to the other, and the dance would stop. Ah, but birth and death continue on our plane, the Sun still turns the Seasons, and the Moon still tugs our Seas and wombs through the Months. These are the signs by which we know that each Pole is equally desirable. Otherwise, there would be no exchange, no rhythm, no dance.

In Wicca's thealogy, the individual lives we're living now are some of many experiences of Individuality that complement our experience of Wholeness. We speak of Wholeness sometimes as the Summerland, and we describe the Summerland with a variety of "sub-metaphors." This is necessary because it's impossible to describe Wholeness in the language of Individuality, just as an expression of Individuality requires distinction from the Whole.

This life is probably not our first, and probably not our last; and in between, we don't have to worry about horrible punishments, for power-over is not Wicca's foundation. At death, we miss

those we're leaving, of course—but this sadness is not thealogically compounded by guilt or fear.

Fear of death is something that Wiccans have been forced to
confront, quite horrifyingly in our legends of the Burning Times,
but in other ways even today. We can consider this heroic, for
death challenges us at the door of the initiatory Circle. This being
the case, death is an admission, in Wicca's symbolic vocabulary, to
the Inner Court. The extreme Inner Court.

Wiccans and other neo-Pagans face fear and loss, and by extension (but sometimes not *much* extension) death, fairly frequently.
Whether or not our mortal lives are threatened by hostile police or
telescopic sights, our economic security is still threatened by our
co-workers' Satanic fantasies. Our civil rights are violated by institutional ignorance and insensitivity, our emotional well-being is rav-
aged by families' and neighbors' cold misunderstandings. Wiccans
and other neo-Pagans face various aspects of death all too often.

I know a few victims of persecution, and none of them would
say they enjoy it, although some of them acknowledge that it can
be exhilarating in a way. None of them, however, have turned
away from Wicca, even though sometimes it looks as though the
Craft is to blame for their problems. Truth to tell, it's not. Ignorance and fear are the root of our problems. How do we get to the
roots of ignorance and fear?

A lot of the love and approval we're offered are conditional.
Many of us have been threatened with separation and taught to
worry about our worthiness. Wicca recognizes that life is a process,
not a single or linear event, and that it is this process of living that
is divine. Life and Death are the complementary poles of energy
by which the process is animated and sustained. Just as the material world in which we adventure is composed of particles and
waves, so *we* are composed of particles and waves; and just as we
see the physical world's particles or waves according to our perspective, so our knowledge of our own forms and natures depends
on our perspectives.

While we are Individual, we interpret the world in the same three dimensions our bodies occupy; and while we are incarnate our concentration is almost *entirely*—but not unshakably—on our perceptions of this state. Individuality (incarnation) is an experience that counterpoints Wholeness, and from it we cannot wholly describe Wholeness. We can only *represent* Wholeness metaphorically and even in Circle, we only skim its surface no matter how deeply we feel we're diving into it.

The model of Wiccan thealogy is a fundamental acknowledgment that Individuals and all the relationships among them, and Individuality's relationship to the Whole, are sacred—and that includes rocks and ocean currents and ants and azaleas and jerks at the office. Wicca can teach us, as we explore it, that *death as an eviction or exile, or as a punishment or any final condition, simply doesn't exist.*

Wicca's heritage is brimming with ballads, legends, and folklore implying reincarnation, echoing the near-death experiences we're familiar with now in largely secular terms. Rebirth is at the core of Wicca's thealogy. Reincarnation is the metaphor for and process by which we are restored to Individuality. Death is the material process by which we are restored to Wholeness. (And we still call orgasm, which affords us a glimpse of Wholeness, the "little death.")

The Goddess promises in Her Charge, ". . . beyond death, I give peace, freedom, and reunion with those who have gone before." The second verse of one of our best-loved and maybe most frequently raised chants goes, "we all die like the Sun God, and like Him we shall return . . ." In short, our liturgical material and our rites and our Elders and our stories teach us that the grave is but a womb, and we believe in some form of reincarnation. So to dread that aspect of life, that side of the spiral we call death, as our culture trains us to do, is painfully confusing to many Wiccans.

Of course, Wicca is not the only religion for which reincarnation is a tenet. Buddhism and Hinduism have always taught reincarnation; the Catholic Church did too, till the sixth century C.E.[2] But Wicca's concept of reincarnation does not encourage us to escape the cycles, or suggest an enlightenment apart from the cycles. Wiccan understandings of reincarnation tend to be in terms of fully experiencing Individuality in all its nearly infinite variety.

There are many ways in which our culture subverts this perfectly reasonable expectation of being reborn. The idea of a never-changing experience of eternity and the idea that all things can be categorized as *either* good *or* evil leaves us with a cultural foundation for zero-sum thinking. Consider this in terms of the half-hour, hour-long or movie-length segments of time in which we now expect to solve our problems these days, the glib sound bytes that have supplanted thoughtful answers to serious questions. Mixed messages to the max. No wonder people fall back to fear.

Our perception, and therefore our understanding, of humanity's interconnectedness with the rest of life on this planet (and the understanding that *systems* and *processes* can be alive too, like the muscles of a great Body) has been distorted. We are too often too easily convinced that the events of our lives—personal, community, national—are singular, without relationship to anything else.

We've learned to accept our society's behavior as if nations' and the planet's systems—economic, weather, socio-cultural, institutional, and others—are unconnected. From that peculiar, dissociated perspective, it's possible to draw the perverse conclusion that we are individually, *personally* unconnected to each other and the rest of life. Clearly intuition, trust, and self-reliance—our natural power, developed over millions of years of evolution—is disrupted by that belief.

We are thus divided, and can be persuaded that there is evidence that Something exists, separate and superior, from which

---

[2]Not until the Second Council of Constantinople, held in 552 C.E., did the Church declare reincarnation heresy.

we are unconnected. If a state and/or religious hierarchy claims regency for that Separate Almighty, *systemic* flaws (over which we have no immediate or practical control) become our *personal* moral faults. Our cultural tendency to personalize systemic flaws has entrenched itself more firmly with each permutation.

Thus developed the expedient social custom of blaming the victim, and it still provides a sort of smoke screen whenever we come too close to wondering if there might not be a better way to handle all of this. "If you didn't have anything to hide, you wouldn't worry about the Authorities' searches." That sort of thinking comes to the rescue of prejudices when they are challenged.

When we speak of assaults like the Inquisition and the Holocaust, it would be insulting to suggest that most victims were happy to play their roles as torturees and martyrs. But surely it's equally outrageous to imagine that they found no comfort in the tenets of their faith. Talking to Bill Moyers long ago on PBS, and using WWII concentration camps as an example, Elie Weisel said, "Victims find no solace in the long run." "Victims are still dead," another participant added a moment later. I couldn't help thinking of "our" victims, the Europeans burned in the Inquisition. Hutton's scholarship shows that historically, the Inquisition's victims weren't Wiccan; but we can still talk about our lore as if it were history, because it helps us clarify and understand our own circumstances. So, those proto-Wiccans we've imagined being imprisoned, tortured, and burned, might *they* have found solace in the long run?

Well, I'd like to think that the idea of reincarnation would have been of some comfort to them, yes. I don't pretend to know exactly how the medieval mind might have understood it: I can't begin to limit my look at the world to medieval science and philosophy! But in Gerald Gardner's quotation from a "seventeenth-century" Book of Shadows, we can see how the first generation of Wiccans thought about it: "you will feel naught, but will go to death and what lies beyond, the Ecstasy of the Goddess." Well, what the Goddess promises in Her Charge, the Ecstasy to which that old Book alluded, is that "beyond death, I give you peace, freedom, and reunion with those who have gone before." This sustains me, and if any Wiccans had faced the Inquisition's fires, I believe they, too, would have found strength in it.

One of modern Wicca's favorite songs, "The Burning Times,"[3] tells of "those who, by the hundreds, holding hands together chose their death in the sea" rather than risk betrayal of their communities under torture, rather than give up their energy to the Inquisition. The modern neo-Pagan belief that death is safe is so strong that we can't help making this fearlessness part of our legends.

Murphy's version of our legend shows us no fear of the pain of dying (though in these days of tubes and wires, there's a healthy fear of the pain of useless, lingering life)—for there are quicker and less demanding ways to end a life than drowning. The association of salt water and the sea with birth and rebirth is not a Jungian invention, either. For coastal Witches the correspondence is plainer than obvious and the symbolism of death in the sea would have been quite clear all 'round.

Indeed, when my dad was dying, he told me that he guessed he needed to "design one more boat." This man spent many years of his life hand-making boats, outrageously small (18-foot) boats that he took out to sea to fish for salmon. He was not a romantic or poetic man, nor one prone to metaphor. That he likened getting his head together about his impending death to designing another boat was, I think, natural for him at a much deeper level than his personality allowed him to acknowledge. Once he'd gotten hold of that metaphor, the panic left his eyes. So yes, I believe that Wicca's approach to death does give solace.

The tenets and perspectives of Wicca have never been hidden. At any and all times and places, all we need to do is look at the

---

[3] A release in 1992 of Charlie Murphy's *Burning Times* was from Ladyslipper Records in Durham, North Carolina. I think it's worth any trouble you have to go to to get it.

world around us. Look closely and you'll see that death is not hidden from us by our Mother, and neither is death a monster in our closet. Mortality is a physical law like gravity, and there is no punishment in it, not when it's in the service of life.

We can also distinguish natural deaths from artificial ones, nourishing deaths from those which are wasteful. Just as every life is unique, so is every death; and we'll make different distinctions between "nourishing" and "wasteful," too. But we all have the capacity to *make* distinctions. Wicca "preaches" personal responsibility, and this is the sort of thing that we must take personal responsibility *for*.

Knowing where the boundaries are between real and artificial—from where you stand—is a lot like having a clear conception, as well as a strong visualization, of what it means to erect a boundary "between the fair and lovely realms we know and the unimaginable realms of the Dread Lords" when we cast our Circles. It's the same sort of poemo-geography. Even more deeply than fractal geometry's landscapes, we and the rest of life, the universe and everything, in all our dimensions, are interconnected. The interconnection is so entire that there is no way to undo it. Cutting the thread of mortality disconnects nothing and no one.

Die we must. "From Me all things proceed, and to Me all things return." This the Goddess states as a fact in Her Charge; but as She asks naught of sacrifice, then this death which is required must not *be* a sacrifice. We use the word nonetheless, modifying it: "willing sacrifice."

Use of the word sacrifice is archaic, maybe. We justify it by recalling its root meaning: "to make sacred," but even so, it conjures up inappropriate images. The concept is easily, sometimes eagerly, misunderstood. The heroic, archetypal death of an individual is more like going enthusiastically to one's destiny—dying doing what s/he loved to do, as they say—than like being thrown, unwilling and terrified, into some hideous pit. It's more like committing to getting married, something that will effect a complete change, largely unknown, in our lives. Yeah, we're a little bit scared, but we go steadfast to the altar anyway. That's sacrifice, if death is. It is the willing exchange of one form for another.

When we talk about deaths like the Kennedys' and Dr. King's, Gandhi's or King Arthur's, it would be nice to have a different word, for these were men who knew that they would—or could—be killed, not just *as* they were doing their life's work, but *because* they were doing their life's work. They accepted dying as a part of their life's work, like you might accept wearing an ugly company tie or commuting 100 miles a day. When dying is part of what you have been called to do, then going to your death isn't giving anything up; it is not a sacrifice, it's an attainment.

I believe that giving up a king or chief represented a significant loss to the tribe, because the dedication of energy wasn't *only* in the dying, and was as much in the surviving. I know it felt that way as this century's leaders were shot down—Gandhi, John F. Kennedy, King, Bobby Kennedy, Sadat. We don't have too much trouble with the idea, though, as long as we're talking about famous people, because we're used to hearing promising young-sters called "the next Somebody Famous." Talking about them isn't the same as talking about ourselves. The idea that dying is part of what Wicca calls *all* of us to do is more difficult.

Being separated from, and thus mistrustful of or unaware of, our instincts and intuition is not very comforting. Bestowed-upon-us righteousness may not have the strength to draw that last inner-directed breath. A hierarchical cosmology that posits a static eternity and eternal judgment doesn't leave us with much hope. But such a faith is not the only form religion can take; it is certainly not the form Wicca has taken.

Wicca's understanding is that time is *cyclical*, not linear. Years are less important than seasons. It is in terms of seasons that we comprehend age, saying we are in the autumn of our life, for instance. Evolution is a manifestation of growth, which is the nature of life, a sort of exemplary sacrament the Goddess declares in Herself.

Death is a stage of growth; Wicca celebrates Samhain as the beginning of a new year because that Sabbat marks the transition of death to conception, the highest magic we know.

The Goddess promises that beyond death we will experience "peace, freedom and reunion with those who have gone before." Generally this is interpreted to mean that when we die, we'll join our uncles and grandmothers and the long-passed animal companions of our youth in the Summerland, where we all go between lives. If death is transformed to conception, then beyond death lies rebirth. Those who have gone before have "gone" not just to the Summerland: they have "gone" back to the *mortal* world before us, too.

This passage in our belovéd Charge asserts reincarnation, not just the peaceful repose we're acculturated to think about. Eternal *anything* doesn't suit Individuality, and nothing in Wiccan liturgy is unilateral. Knowing that the energy goes both ways, knowing that *our* energy goes both ways, it makes sense to care about the future, because we'll be coming back to it. It's not futile to initiate or work on projects we won't see finished in this life, because we will enjoy their completion in another. We *are* the future generations.

One doesn't have to remember past lives to have lived them. The simple physical truth is that there's a finite amount of material with which to make stuff—rocks, clouds, azaleas, wombats, people. Every molecule that's here now, in your body, in the paper upon which this book is printed, and in the air you're breathing, is made of bits that have been around since the Big Bang (the Goddess's *OH!*). All these molecules can be matter, or they can be transformed into energy, and back again to matter ("everything is everything," as you'll remember from the 60s), but you can't go anywhere and come back with *more* matter or *more* energy.

The universe is a giant recycling plant—and it's not only perfectly reasonable, it's absolutely necessary to reuse matter and energy. That is, when something passes out of material existence back into the energy matrix, some of its atoms and waves may be of immediate use in the creation of something else material. When you knock down one block castle, you use the same blocks to build another. Not every material disintegration is so thorough as to produce energy; most often, material disintegration is only partial, and the leavings are still molecular. Are you wearing any gold jewelry? Chances are it has a fleck or two of Pharaoh's gold in it, and that's reincarnation too.

Even if your memory doesn't hold any coherent understanding of past lives, you've been here for a long time. Your molecules are native, and came from the bones and veins and dreams of people and clouds and leaves that have come and gone a hundred times. You're an heirloom. Reincarnation—whether you understand it biochemically, in a physicist's terms, metaphorically as a sort of literary aspect of life, or spiritually—is the way of the Worlds. Wiccan thealogians explain it with many analogies, and we are in agreement that it is a fact of life.

Now, our physical bodies are made up of matter. Our auric bodies are composed of energy. When our souls leave our bodies, the physical body decomposes as matter will; our auric bodies also gradually decompose, their energies redistributed. When the energies that formed your auric bodies is released, it may become part of another aura without completely disintegrating (forgetting) first. When you knock down one block castle, remember, you're using at least some of the same blocks in the next one you build, and something about the one you build next may well remind you of one you built before.

Do you believe in ghosts? My son asked me that once and I said that I did, in the same way and for the same reason that I believe in echoes and after-images. I've told him that ghosts are either unconscious left-over energy that needs to be grounded, or a confused consciousness that needs a little help completing the death experience, needs to be "settled," they used to say. In *Stroking the Python*, Diane Stein says that ghosts are "retrocognitive thought-forms."[4] This makes sense to me. You might say, too, that ghosts are projections of the Akashic Record. Less elegantly, you could say that ghosts are the traces of human lives and emotions, and our perceiving them ought not to seem any more amazing than a bloodhound's following a scent.

Place-ghosts, the kind that haunt houses and jinx possessions, fascinate everybody, and many people think they're malevolent, or at least mischievous. In fact, I think this must be in the eyes of the beholders, because place-ghosts are stuck, their energy hasn't cleared the plane, and their preoccupation with whatever event or circumstance traps them is utter. They don't warn or intimidate, they just recur. I think that if these ghosts are aware of us at all, they are only drawn to our incarnate-ness, as a wandering amnesiac might think for a moment that this house, or that one, might be the lost home.

Sometimes by careful intervention it's possible to lay, or settle, these ghosts, to interact with the left-over energy and allow it to ground. Our own reaction to seeing or sensing a ghost might be so unpleasant as to feel like malice, but it is unlikely that a place-ghost would be "interactively responsive" to anything in the material here and now. The ghost's concern is with the environment and situation that compel it, and anything it does or says is then and there, not here and now.

Independent ghosts, on the other hand, can be purposeful. They may appear to us because our emotional state draws them. Our "vibes" can attract harmonious and sympathetic energies, I think: our animal companions and other people we know can "tell how we feel," because energy is sensitive to energy. If we can approach a weeping stranger to offer aid and comfort, then ghost-strangers can approach us, I trust. They appear for other reasons too, and can interact with us to some extent, audially and visually. They

[4]Diane Stein, *Stroking the Python: Women's Psychic Lives* (Llewellyn Publications, St. Paul, 1988), 213.

can warn us of danger or opportunity, they can bring news, they can suggest answers to problems we face.

It is possible, I suppose, for such ghosts to be malicious or vengeful, but malice and vengeance are both high-energy intents, and ghosts do not have an unlimited supply of energy. (Correspondingly, it takes more muscles, and thus more energy, to frown than it does to smile.) To maintain an Earth-tie, without a physical body, while supporting a strong negative emotion would drain most auras within a generation, I should think—unless there was a handy supply of energy in a usable form; fear doesn't feed the fiends in folklore for nothing!

The Wiccan Sabbat at Samhain honors the dead at a feast that is something like a family reunion. We do not make offerings to propitiate our ghosts. We share our harvest with them. We affirm that they're still influential in our lives, and we affirm our faith that the grave is a womb and that the life cycle really is a *life cycle*. So Wiccans aren't afraid of ghosts. We feel the same kinship with them that we do with any life or aspect of life. Working with a ghost, helping to ground its energy, is no more spooky or unnatural than working with your kid through adolescence or your spouse through a mid-life crisis. "Ghost" is a stage through which not *everything* passes, but even so, it is a *natural* state, and not one to hold against anybody who does go through it.

I've never met anyone who used to be Napoleon—or Josephine, or anybody else famous. Most people who recall past lives recall relative humility. The point in past-life recall is in fact not to have been somebody famous, but to learn something that will make growth easier in *this* life. Having been a Caesar won't buy pizza, but maybe remembering what it was like to be harassed as a medieval cripple will inspire a brilliant architectural access design.

My *personal* sense of it is that there are as many styles of reincarnation as there are styles of incarnation. I read somewhere that the Irish Druids believed that you could choose whether and when to return. Some say once a human, always a human, while others insist that you can come back as a snake or a tree. (I must say that I vehemently disagree with those who believe that coming back as anything other than human is a step down. I think that would be sideways, not down, and lateral thinking is touted as the most creative.)

I think that if you can keep your consciousness together, you have full freedom of choice; if you drift away or divide into aspects, then you'll find yourself put to use as needed. Looking at it like that, it's easy to see what we call "death" as a lot like getting off the train at your home station after a really long and great trip. You're tired, wobbly, and glad to be back; you need a minute to sort it out and put the snapshots in order. If you aren't sure who you are or what your pictures are of, don't worry, somebody remembers, and the God/ess will love you anyhow. And whatever "putting the snapshots in order" means, in the Summerland you'll have plenty of time.

When we die, we conventionally expect to join our loved ones in the Summerland, where we all go between lives. But those who have gone before may "go" back to the mortal world "before" too. Are our forebears here with us?

Of course they are with us in our *memories* of them, but is little Davey really great-uncle Meerschaum reincarnate? Only the people who know Davey and knew Uncle Meerschaum should venture an opinion about that. Certainly the reports of fairly immediate reincarnations, in time for friends of the deceased to meet her again, are the most spectacular, and the easiest to record and investigate.

But it is not my impression that "most" reincarnation is immediate. After all, it's not the case that most mammals, say, have similar life spans. Some of us live a hundred years, some of us live for three. Does that mean that the long-lived specimens or short-lived specimens are freaks? Of course, neither are freaks—and so it should not seem unusual if some souls are reincarnated sooner than others. We living things add a lot of different rhythms to the cosmic harmony.

Nobody knows exactly *how* reincarnation actually *works*, although lots of people have pretty specific ideas. Is it a problem to accept reincarnation without knowing how it works? I don't think so. We accept lots of things without knowing exactly how they work. Gravity, for instance, and magnetism and electricity. I for one would be hard pressed to explain an internal combustion engine, much less build one; but I drive one when I need to. No one can tell you how to interpret the principle of reincarnation, but most Wiccan clergy will tell you that this principle is one of the ancient foundations of the faith.

Reincarnation is Nature's example generally, and in various forms it has been a tenet of most human faiths, globally and throughout history. It is central to Wicca and other initiatory religions.[5] Scientific observation, exploration, and examination of the universe has not contradicted the idea.

We don't have many ways to "measure" reincarnation right now, no standardized scientific method of testing an asserted case. Much of the evidence is anecdotal and subjective, and our either/or upbringing urges us to disregard that evidence specifically because it *can't* be measured with any instruments we have today. Besides, concepts of reincarnation challenge the permanence of any afterlife and the finality of any judgment. Those challenges are still intolerable to large segments of the status quo: not just to religious hierarchies, but to political and economic blocs and institutions as well.

Yet because Wicca rests on personal responsibility, each of us has to decide what evidence to consider, and how to weigh it, how to understand it. Reincarnation has been a cornerstone of many human faiths, and it is a cornerstone for Wicca as well. But

---

[5] Most Native traditions—anywhere—are initiatory. Even religions that don't call themselves initiatory tend to have initiatory elements in their ordination rituals. Catholics give some of their clerics new names, for instance.

Wicca does not definitively interpret reincarnation—or any tenet of the faith—for us. That's because Witchcraft is a religion of experience, not commandments. It would be inconsistent, and I think unnecessary, for our priestesses and priests to tell us what to believe, for Witches follow a path of self-discovery. "That which you do not find within," the Goddess warns us, "you shall surely never find without."

Without you will find a hundred possibilities, three hundred, three hundred zillion. Only within will you find *your* belief, *your* path, and *your* life, this time and next.

Ritual and Magic

Ritual is the means by which a community can share experience and build a common vision of the world on the *group's* interpretation of the *group's* experience. The lives of individuals have meaning in the groups they create; as above, so below: Individuality (that which dies and is reborn) finds its meaning in relationship to Wholeness.

When we do solitary rituals, our Individuality complements the Goddess's Wholeness; when we do ritual in covens or groves or festivals, all of us together signify the Whole, and our individual self-lives are rich with meaning in *that* context. Once again, as above, so below: our covens and other groups are symbolic of the Whole from which Individuality is born, the Whole that Individuality informs and enriches. We are meant to relate to our covens (and other groups) in ways that describe our relationships with Life, the Universe, and Everything.[1] The relationships we create and nurture on this plane are models of the relationships we expect on other planes.

The rituals we make around death are like any other rituals: they enlarge shared experience and its value, they affirm our common visions and *their* value, as well as expanding our individual worth in wider contexts. In ritual we participate in an altered

---

[1] I use this phrase often. It comes from Douglas Adams's "five-part trilogy," *The Hitchhiker's Guide to the Galaxy*. Science fiction influences Witches, and Wicca, and offers some really helpful models. One of the ways I think about the experience of death, for instance, is in terms of the Total Perspective Vortex that Zaphod Beeblebrox survived with flying colors.

reality which we are sharing by consensus. Dying, it is difficult to be active in that consensus; we must rely upon our friends to hold reality steady for us, as we'd expect them to hold the ladder still while we climb to the roof.

It is important that our death rituals be attentive to the specific needs of the person who is dying. As attendants, it is our task to be the solid ground from which our dying friend can embark on the return trip to Wholeness. It is for us not only to feed the cats when our friend is gone, but also, to an appropriate degree, to keep our friend focused on—reminded and assured about—the journey s/he is undertaking.

We know that we are not our bodies, any more than we are the cars that carry us around town and country. Yet we must pay attention to our body's responses, just as we have to keep an eye on the car's gauges. And though we may rationally expect both our bodies and our cars to be ready for trade-in one day, we still might be distressed when that time comes.

It's hard work to personalize death rituals; it's emotionally challenging and socially intimidating. Yet unpersonalized, the ritual may not be successful, and given that a death ritual is the last one our belovéd can share with us, there's a very strong need to "get it right." (But hey, no pressure!) Can it be done? Can there be a perfect death ritual? Well, no, there can't be *a* perfect death ritual, not just one that will be just right for everybody who dies. But yes, you can create a death ritual that's just what it should be for the person you have in mind, whether that's yourself or someone else. The question isn't so much whether you can create an appropriate ritual, as how you should go about it.

The first thing to do, I think, is to be aware of the feelings that need to be acknowledged. We are talking about ritual acknowledgment here, but dying people also need ordinary acknowledgment of their feelings. Remember that the Goddess takes all acts of love and pleasure for rituals, and know that through the pain of openly sharing someone else's distress you will learn deeper Mysteries.

Fear? Not everyone feels it, and let's hope you and yours don't. But if it is an element of someone's experience, you will need to address it. Ritual is a safe place to acknowledge fear because in ritual the fear can be *resolved*.[2] If it's a carefully designed ritual, it will not only help people to magically ground fear, it may also suggest some practical applications.

One feeling that almost everybody seems to encounter is anger. According to Elisabeth Kübler-Ross, anger is a typical response to death, whether you're the one doing the dying or the one doing the staying behind. Most people have trouble handling their own anger or anybody else's on a good day, and it's not usually a good day if somebody you care about is dying.[3] So anger may need to be addressed ritually, too. This can be done in many ways: it can be done in ritual drama, where people's own anger can be dissipated with their character's, and it can be done in dancing and it can be done in chanting and it can be done in simple, honest statements.

But ritual must do more than ground us. Ritual must also reorient us. When we're doing death, we are deep between the Worlds and we emerge to a *changed* mundane environment. We're often disoriented by the changes and we rely on ritual to help us reinterpret our environment. It is as if a fundamental landmark has disappeared from the physical landscape. While the difference between what we expect to see and what we do see still boggles us, we need help finding our way around.

In the same way, when somebody dies, we need help reformulating the meaning of life, the meaning of *our* lives. Our brain chemistry has turned us inward, probably with some suddenness and strength, and we feel disoriented. Ritual helps us find our bearings again. Quite literally, in one sense: of course the Circle

---

[2] Some of the guided meditations in Diane Mariechild's *MotherWit* (The Crossing Press, Freedom, CA, 1981) are good for this.

[3] We've all heard, though, about warriors of many cultures setting out to battle affirming that today is a great day to die. It's hard to get to that perspective, but most heroes aim for it.

orients us to the planet's directions. But the Circle also reorients us to the Wheel, to the cycle, to the process. Death is one of those awesome transitions that dazzles us, entrances us, concentrates our focus so sharply that it's easy to forget it is not all there is to see.

Additionally, ritual reorients us to our community, shows us that we still belong, that we are not alone even though we are turned so inward that we might *feel* alone. Sometimes alone is how we need to feel, the long hall down which we need to walk to an important room or space within ourselves. Ritual holds us and rocks us in belonging, and rebirths us from our sympathetic journey to the Underworld.

Let me make it clear that ritual is not all we need. Simple friendship is crucial. When I was in Oregon, tending by myself to my father while he died, preoccupied as I was by that work, I could physically feel the energy my friends in Tucson were sending. It had a physical effect not unlike that of aspirin, and an emotional effect not unlike being sung to sleep. There's more we can do for each other when we're grieving, too. Beyond the immediate sympathy and support we can offer and receive, an extended tolerance of exhaustion and witlessness is helpful.

People in transition (infancy, adolescence, parenthood, menopause, death) can get "mush-brained." It's at least partly hormonal, and it temporarily reduces our left-brain skills. It's useful in that it focuses us on the biochemical task at hand. Some cultures take the strange behavior that often characterizes transitions as sacredly meaningful. Other cultures call it crazy and try to suppress it. Friends try to see the creativity in it, and don't let the mush-brainer hurt herself.

It is natural for us, psycho-spiritually, to share experiences. Empathy is an evolutionarily useful capacity, and it may be empathically that we withdraw from the ordinary world when someone close to us dies. Grief is a shamanistic experience, and in shamanistic journeys there is a sense of cycle, and a time to return to the world of light and matter. For someone who has died, the cycle has lengthened, not stopped.

Ritual with a group of people is both help on the journey back and celebration of safe return; and in being both is an affirmation of the process, the cycle. If the mourners symbolize the one who has died, then a ritual can welcome the mourners back to the wider community and also presage and energize the rebirth of our loved one. Indeed, an important part of any death ritual is the affirmation of rebirth, for that affirmation is itself a work of sympathetic magic.

Such rites have been sung and danced for death forever. There can be no question that since we've been human we've been in awe of death and birth. The life-force has always been revered equally with elemental forces, and even now confounds science as thoroughly as they do. But Wiccans need not be confounded. Wiccan thealogy offers a fearless, nonviolent model of deity and a world view which gives great comfort and does not discount our experience and perception. Wicca is participatory: no sitting on hard benches to hear from *anyone* the unquestionable word of an unearthly god for us, and no isolation with only an illusion or divine dream for company! No, we sing, feast, and dance, we make music and love, all in Her presence—and all in the presence of our belovéd dead, too.

Wiccan thealogy offers us magic as a reality. Sometimes in sadness and the other dimensions of grief, we forget the magic. Remember it. Most of us have heard the scientific community affirm that touching heals. Babies die if we don't hold them. Spirits die if bodies don't hug. We know from experience that after an argument, a together-hug restores calmness and confidence to our body chemistry. Death, the journey to the Summerland, and the initial reunion—a together-hug with the Gods—restores calmness and confidence to our life chemistry. In both cases, consciousness is changed. Magic, according to writer Dion Fortune, is the art of changing consciousness *at will*.

Every blink, every breath, every thought, every relationship changes our chemistry. Our brain chemistry rather directly reflects our inner explorations. Everything we do, no matter which plane we do it on, changes our brain chemistry. (This would include, for instance, changes resulting from the physical act of reading this book, and changes that result from thinking about what you read.) In every experience, some changes are subtle, some are not. They're all magic.

If we have deduced and accepted that our physical characteristic of having opposable thumbs implies that we are "meant to" use tools, why is it so difficult to deduce and accept that our physical characteristic of constantly changing consciousness implies a use for *that* capacity? It's reasonable to think that one underlying purpose of our cerebral cortex is to enable our awareness to survive death. Perhaps the primal capacity to create thought forms was a capacity to hold individual consciousnesses together through nonmaterial phases.

Today's magic is, of course, what's left of these original native capacities. Our understanding of them now is still limited, but we still have the precious ancestral heirloom tool, our *trust*. What's lost can be restored, recreated. Our sense of death as a sort of birthrite, an Initiation for which our life has been the ritual preparation, can be restored to us too, if we understand that we lost it unnaturally, to power-over.

That single misperception—that life, the universe, and everything is driven by power-over—has narrowed our minds and consequently diminished our capacities. Magic gives us the experience of other perspectives. Magic lets us see that power-over is not the cosmic way. Our sense of balance requires us to tune ourselves to the cosmic chords, not random quarter notes.

Embodied and disincarnate, life is just doing what it has always done: cycling through the polarity, now energy, now matter, now active, now receptive, now individual, now reintegrated, now infinitely dense, now expanding forever. What once was the corona of a sun may now be glistening in a baby's smile. Magic. There's matter and there's energy, and many manifestations of each. But those two states are all there is, and they complement (rather than oppose) each other. Together they are one, and more than one.

Witches also understand ritual in terms of energy exchange, and it is possible to send energy to spirits to help them finish dying. Most cultures have some idea that a soul, once disincorporated, has places to go and things to do. Most cultures have some experience of those souls being distracted by the leaving-the-body part of death. Ritual can be of real help to someone who has died, then, by transmitting energy that will reorient the misdirected soul.

This is fundamental to the death rites of many Eastern religions, and there are strong if not straightforward hints of it in Western legends as well. But the West is mostly still wary of the idea that we can actively participate in death, from either side. The idea is not alien to Wicca, though. It is hardly even an extension of our usual magic to send energy to our recently dead lovers and friends, energy that will guide them, strengthen them for their journey. Doing ritual to such a purpose helps not only the soul on the way to the Summerland, but also the mourners, when our understanding of death as a journey needs reinforcement in the saddest moments of our grief.

(I'll sound one caution here. After the terrorist attacks of September 11, 2001, lots of people, including Wiccans, "sent energy" to the victims. My coven raised and sent "carry on" energy to the survivors, for rebuilding of high-rises and hearts. At Samhain, we remembered the victims and wished them fair progress on their own paths. We felt it was unethical to wish them well on their way to Summerland, when most of them had other destinations in mind. Even when the dying are our own friends and families, we must respect their different beliefs, and lend our support to *their* metaphors. That way, we truly honor our loved ones, and then we can reasonably expect our friends and families to respect and honor our beliefs and customs.)

How long should a ritual last? Well, that depends, among other things, on who will be attending. If everybody's an Initiate or an apprentice, it might go on for several hours, or several days, or adjourn and reconvene several times over a period of days or months. If there are many *cowan* (non-Wiccan) in attendance, the ritual might be shorter, more like a conventional funeral, with some of its witchier elements reserved for more private remembrances; or it might be conducted in more than one part; or some provision might be made to teach the cowan how to honor the Wiccan who has died.

The style in which anyone is remembered should be harmonious with the way they lived, so it'll be different for everybody. Wiccan requiems are very personal—there will never be a single ritual that's repeated in exactly the same way by every coven on the planet, just as there will never be a single universal ritual for any Sabbat or Esbat. Even when we have copies of requiem rites, we're bound and inclined to modify them to fit the instant need. Wicca's participatory ritual form and structure, which *is* universally shared among the Craft's denominations, developed as the most conservative—that is, energy-efficient—way of maintaining and directing the energy that we raise in traditional worship and celebration.

The Wiccan Circles we cast today are well-suited to contain and work creatively with the energy generated by our hearts and minds when someone dies. And of course we have models for our requiems in more than one Sabbat theme: Lammas and Mabon and Samhain leap to mind. At the deaths of our friends as well as at certain Sabbats, our duty, if I may presume to say so, is to acknowledge the service the Dying One has given to life, and to reaffirm rebirth. Every Sabbat is its own point on the Wheel and yet directs our attention to its complement as well; every death reassures us that we will be born again.

Emotions run high when someone is dying. Without the extra energy our feelings generate, we wouldn't be able to accomplish the tasks a death requires of us, individually and communally.

Wiccan funeral rites do not deny any feelings. In a Wiccan requiem there is room for personal expressions of grief, even unusual ones. A Klingon death-howl rose from one requiem Circle here some years ago, and rose with dignity because it was raised in love.

Wiccan requiems are conducted by friends, family, coven, lovers, children—and the participation is energizing, empowering. It is a way to reaffirm our connection with the deceased, to resolve the painfully apparent distinction between life and death through ritual, which is the spiritual language that translates among the material and the nonmaterial realms. Can we go beyond our youthful focus on our bodies, on the physical world, to explore the other realms that are open to us? Are we willing to die to be reborn? Wicca lets us answer *yes!*

Some death rituals have been published. For instance, Delia Morgan's beautiful solitary ritual is in *The Family Wicca Book*;[4] Paul V. Beyerl's seven-day Rowan Tree rite is in *A Wiccan Bardo*;[5] and Starhawk and her friends' *The Pagan Book of Living and Dying*[6] offers additional material. There are more ideas in this book, too. Most manuals, including Buckland's[7] and the Farrars',[8] outline death rituals. Many Traditions make their rituals available on an individual basis if you ask nicely.

It would be the best thing, though, for us each to write our *own* rituals. Failing that, it would be good if we could all outline our own rituals; and if that seems too much, at least write down

---

[4]Ashleen O'Gaea, *The Family Wicca Book: the Craft for Parents and Children* (Llewellyn, St. Paul, 1993).

[5]Paul V. Beyerl, *A Wiccan Bardo: Initiation and Self-Transformation* (Prism Press, Bridport, Dorset, England, 1989; in the U.S., Avery Publishing Group).

[6]Starhawk and M. Macha Nightmare and the Reclaiming Collective, *The Pagan Book of Living and Dying: Practical Rituals, Prayers, Blessings, and Meditations on Crossing Over* (Harper-SanFrancisco, 1997).

[7]Raymond Buckland, *Buckland's Complete Book of Witchcraft* (Llewellyn Publications, St. Paul, 1986).

[8]Janet and Stewart Farrar, *A Witches Bible Complete* (Magickal Childe, New York, 1984).

your favorite chants and quotations and give somebody a clue about what you'd like done with your body and where you'd like it to end up.

"We all come from the Goddess, and to Her we shall return/ like a drop of rain, flowing to the ocean." Shall your friends make a pilgrimage to the seashore and scatter your ashes there? Maybe toast you and chant for you around a driftwood fire?

"We all die like the Sun-god, and like Him we are reborn—like a spark of flame, rising up forever." Shall your friends construct an honorable effigy and burn it on a pyre, doing the ancient circle dance in affirmation of the Spiral?

Do you have a favorite chant, a line or two of the Charge that comforts you? Did you read something once that hit home a little more than everything else? Is there a sound or an image, that is so meaningful to you it could be a symbol to remember you by? If it occurs to you that there is, *tell somebody now*. Put this book down and write it down or call a friend right now.

How about a meditation, a guided journey to a different level of the Underworld, a sort of walking to the end of the pier so your friends can have a longer time to wave goodbye. (I read, back in April or May of 1998, that Paul McCartney led his belovéd Linda on a guided horseback meditation ride as she died.) "Beyond death, I give peace, and freedom, and reunion with those who have gone before." Shall your friends each take the part of someone you loved who died earlier, and all of them act out your welcome in the Summerland?

Following are several rituals and other liturgical pieces addressing various aspects of the death experience. These are offered as ideas, models, examples, and they're meant to be modified and borrowed from and rearranged in whatever ways you find most useful. It is certainly important to ground our rituals in our communal ethno-ancestral past, and in the several centuries of Wicca's British heritage. But it is equally important to let our immediate environments and experiences be reflected in our rituals, too.

All the rituals in this chapter are more or less traditionally structured, and draw freestyle upon Anglo-Celtic images. These rituals are eclectic, partly because Campsight Coven is eclectic within Adventure's parameters, and partly because *life* is eclectic.

Because all these rituals are concerned with the transition we call death, they all take celebrants through a whole transition or accomplish a full integration. In practice, these completions may not be noted on the conscious level, may be taken for granted, just as casting and closing are not always remarkable in Circle. On the inner levels of consciousness, though, the closure is duly noted and the magic duly set to work.

Most of these rituals require personalization, an individual's active participation. The practical need for this is obvious, but there is a deeper purpose served, for intimate participation in the ritual is an invitation to enter the Underworld, to risk . . . ah, to risk finding out the Horrible Truth about yourself?

No! Rather, to risk finding out that, as Brooke Medicine Eagle paraphrased a friend saying to her, "You're all magnificent, trying to be okay." In the Adventure tradition, the way you proceed on your Quest is by accepting those invitations, those magical dares. When you are sure of yourself, you can recognize everybody else as magnificent too, and furthermore, you can recognize all the paths (almost) by which people travel as equally worthy.

Adventure's metaphors let us say this: when our Quest companions die, they disappear 'round a bend on a path down which the main party will not follow now. We all come to our own crossroads and leave the main company behind. Eventually, we all gather again in the mead-hall of some great king or queen, perhaps one of those with whom we walk today.

And 'midst the toasts and the platters and the shouts of recognition, we will tell our stories, sing our songs, and recite the names of our parents and of our children. We will reveal our discoveries and compare our magics, and we will make plans to set out again on new adventures, perhaps as companions again, perhaps with a vow to meet at the old place in the usual span of years, there to raise the toasts again.

When you find out that someone you care about is dying, or has died, you're shaken to the core, and that's true whether the "someone" is human or not. Other major changes can shake you, too: divorce, unemployment, your move to a new place, or somebody else's move away. When that happens, you need to get grounded. If you are facing the experience of death, yourself or with somebody else, it's *especially* important to reaffirm your own relationship to the Gods, because your patterns of relationship here in the ordinary world are destabilized when somebody dies. And it may very well be the case that *you're* the one on whom everybody *else* wants to rely.

When you're as aware as death makes you of the temporal nature of life here on Planet Earth, you need to reconnect firmly with that which is eternal and generative—the Goddess—and you need equally firmly to reconnect the idea of *rebirth* with the idea of death. This ritual, easy to modify according to personal circumstances, is designed with those needs in mind.

Because the circumstances surrounding death and other losses and changes vary widely, so you may need to shorten, or you may be able to lengthen, this ritual. You can combine it or parts of it with other rituals, too; and do it as elaborately or simply as you like.

The Affirmation of the Flowers

Preparation

For this ritual you will need a packet of flower seeds and two small candles, one to represent you and one to represent your loss. If you have time and are inclined, feel free to use novelty candles in any shapes that seem appropriate to you. You will also need your personal calendar and something to write with, *and* you will need a cauldron or bowl in which to make a small fire, and another small bowl.

Set your altar up as you normally do, except that you should use a rainbow or multi-colored altar cloth, or several overlapping cloths of different colors; and even if you don't normally use a bell in your rites, you'll need one this time. You will also need anointing (Goddess) oil.

Before you start, cut out the picture on the front of the seed packet; keep the planting instructions with you and pour the seeds into the small bowl.

Your cakes and ale should be something you really enjoy, so that you're not just going through the motions when you feast, even though you might find your appetite is slightly depressed when you are shocked or grieving. Something sweet or some nuts will help.

Finally, before you begin, cleanse yourself. It is best in these circumstances to take a full bath or shower, and it is very comforting to do that in candlelight and with gentle incense.

The Ritual

Cast your Circle in your most formal way. Speak and walk slowly and let your gestures and inflections be broad and dramatic.

Invoke the Goddess and the God namelessly, only by description and epithet. You may wish to do this spontaneously, or write something out ahead of time; reading it is fine. Campsight's invocations, though short, are suitable examples here:

Great Mother, Triple Brigit, reaver and bereaved, comfort me with Your blessings on this Circle and its Work.

Wild Brother, Lover, slayer and slain, comfort me with Your blessings on this Circle and its Work.

When you feel the Gods respond to your invocations, take your time at each Quarter, focusing on the correspondences and images of your calls. When the Circle is cast, thrice declare yourself between the Worlds, ringing the bell *before and after* each declaration.

Now that you are between the Worlds, anoint the candle that represents your loved one or your loss. As you do this, focus on the cauldron you've brought into the Circle, and meditate on it as the Womb. When you are done, set that candle in the cauldron, light it, and ring the bell.

Now anoint the candle that represents you, again focusing on the cauldron and meditating on rebirth. When you are ready, light your candle from the one that's already burning in the cauldron, set it in the cauldron an inch or so away from the first candle (if your cauldron's not big enough, position the candles so that they appear and seem to you distinct rather than merging) and ring the bell again.

Taking up the front of the seed packet, carry that picture of blooming flowers around to each Quarter. Hold the picture up to each Quarter and say,

"Every year the Earth rejoices in the return of life, every year the Earth is reborn, every year the fields prosper anew. Even so did I rejoice in _____ and even so was I reborn in sharing life and love and beauty with _____."

Bring the picture back to the center. Crumple it slightly and say,

"But blooms fade, leaves fall, and stems and roots bow to harvest."

Ring the bell. Drop the crumpled flower-picture into the cauldron and let it burn. If you like, purify yourself with that smoke, but be aware that it will probably not smell good.

When there is nothing left of the flowers but the shiny ashes, the two candles should still be burning. If they are not, light them again, yours with the Goddess candle from the altar, the other with the God candle. Then take up the bowl with the seeds in it.

Take these seeds around to each Quarter. Holding the bowl up to each Quarter, say,

"There is no harvest without seed for another planting; there is no death without rebirth. Even as _____ has died, _____ shall be reborn. Even as these seeds will bring the flowers back to life, so will _____ pass again through the Door that opens upon Youth."

Come back to the cauldron in the center and set the bowl of seeds down in front of it, and ring the bell. Hold the bowl over the cauldron and say,

"This is the Door that opens upon Youth, and by the power of the Earth, these dead seeds shall be returned to life. By the power of the Mother's Womb, all that dies is reborn. And as I will recognize these flowers and rejoice in them again when they return from the Underworld, so do I know that _____ will return, for it is the nature of life to die and be reborn."

Ring the bell.

Now, read the back of the seed packet and count down the weeks on your calendar and make a mark—not with words, just a magical mark—at the day or week when the seeds in the bowl will sprout. In the air over the bowl, with your finger, make the same magical sign over the seeds. Say,

"There is no death without rebirth. The grave is but a womb. As _____ was committed to the grave, so _____ was committed to rebirth and has been reconceived in the Womb of Life. Magic will bring these seeds to life, and that magic is the sign by which we all shall be reborn.

"I bless these seeds in memory of _____, and when they sprout, I will recognize the magic and know that _____ is safe and will one day be reborn as these flowers are reborn.

"I bless these seeds in memory of joy and friendship. In perfect love and perfect trust do I bless these seeds, knowing that they will come to life as all things are brought to life through death. And when these seeds have been reborn, the joy and friendship I knew with _____ will be reborn in me as well, for it is the nature of life to die and be reborn."

Ring the bell.

Now bless your cakes and ale in your usual way, eat and drink everything you have brought into the Circle, saving only a little bit for the cauldron (or your usual libation bowl, if you have one). With your offering and libation, ring the bell.

Close your Circle in the usual way, but (especially if you are with other people) don't say the "Merry meet" yet. First, go outside and plant those seeds according to the instructions on the seed packet. Say your "Merry meet" as you plant the seeds; and when they sprout, remember to say, "Merry meet again."

Here is a shorter piece to memorize or read or copy out or otherwise remember is true for all of us.

A Private Affirmation

When I am delighted, there are hearts to share my pleasure;
When I am troubled, there are hearts to comfort me.
When I find my way there are hands to take mine in
    congratulation;
When I stray from my path there are hands to draw me back.
When my cup runneth over there are jugs mine can fill;
When my cup is empty, there are jugs within my reach.
When my thoughts are bright, there are minds I can enlighten;
When my thoughts are discouraged,
there are minds to share wonder with me.
I am alive and I am in the Circle. I am unique, but I am not
    alone.

(Winter 1984)

Even when a death is what we can call "timely," when the life has been long and full, we like some reassurance that it isn't really *over*. It isn't. The soul of the person we love will go on to other experience, on other planes. The following ritual helps to reaffirm that for those of us left behind on this plane. You will need to find out if it is feasible where you live; in some states, it may not be, because it makes use of sparklers. Yes, just like the ones you may have waved around on the Fourth of July when you were a child. (If sparklers are illegal where you live, look for trick birthday candles that won't blow out.)

Preparation

Sparklers come in different colors: gold, silver, red, blue, green. You'll want to choose an appropriate color—or you may want to combine them. As long as you are careful, there's no reason not to use more than one. You will also need a cauldron. Even though you'll be using sparklers in this ritual, you can use a plastic cauldron, the kind they sell at the "five and dimes" around Halloween every year, if it's big enough. (The biggest I've found measures almost a foot at the opening.) Finally, you'll need a doll, play-figure, or poppet to represent the deceased, and some cloth to shroud the doll. The sparklers, if possible, should be hidden in the cauldron before anyone else arrives.

The Ritual

When the Circle has been cast and all the participants are ready, consecrate the cloth with Salt and Water. Everyone present should take part in shrouding the doll with this cloth. Maybe the priestess or priest can wrap it, and everyone else can hold it for a moment, breathing onto it or otherwise personally blessing it; or maybe all hands can take part in the wrapping, much as all hands may touch the bread for the blessing.

Next, the doll is "buried" in the cauldron, to appropriate words and chants. As this is being done, any electric lights in the room should be turned off, and as soon as the "body" is committed to the cauldron, the Circle's candles, too, should be extinguished, deosil (clockwise) from the South, with East the last one to go out.

After observing a few moments of silence, the priestess or priest should reach into the cauldron and *with extreme care* light the sparkler, so that it's blazing when it emerges. It may be that no one will want or be able to speak at this point, and that's alright. Words about sparkling memories and dazzling new truths would be appropriate, of course, but the sparklers will speak for themselves; or you may wish to start the "Hecaté, Cerridwen (Dark Mother let us in/let us be reborn)" chant before lighting the sparklers, and let it continue while they burn. You will know the right ways to modify this ritual for someone you love.

When the sparkler has burned out, put the wires back in the cauldron. If you have not chanted yet, begin the "Hecaté, Cerridwen" chant now; or use "We all die like the Sun God" if you feel it's more appropriate. Recall, when you can (over cakes and ale is nice), how the deceased shone in your lives—and how s/he always will, because even though bodies die, light and life are eternal.

This is a simple ritual, and though you can put words to it, it is equally powerful conducted almost silently. Many variations are possible, of course: you could chant the dead person's name or Circle name, or you could release your grief atonally.

Another way to affirm the Wiccan expectation that our loved ones—and we!—will be reborn is to ask each of the assembled mourners to contribute something to a packet of "grave goods," which is then "buried" with the poppet in the cauldron as described above. After grief has been expressed—perhaps even by howling, although you may need to find quieter ways if there are neighbors who might be alarmed—a different poppet can be produced from the cauldron, or the same poppet can be taken out and unshrouded, born again as all our loved ones will be. A single black candle, burning throughout the ritual to represent the transformation of grave to womb, might then be used to light a multi-colored or birthday candle representing rebirth. If the poppet you've used is actually a doll, then you should consider giving it away so that a child you never meet can play with it.

Perhaps each of the mourners would like to take home from the bag of grave goods a tool or memento different from the one s/he contributed, and take it home not only as a remembrance of the person who has died, but as a reminder that s/he "only goes the way we all go by, by and by."[9] (Of course, you can put grave goods in the coffin or grave, or you could leave them as an offering near the burial place or where the cremains are kept or scattered.)

We all need to acknowledge that while we may not meet our loved ones again in this life, that does not mean they will not be reborn while we are still alive; nor does it mean that they will not be loved or cared for if they do not meet us again right away. Life is a spiral, not a linear, back-and-forth game of Pong.

One of the most difficult deaths to cope with is that of a child. If your child or one of the children in your family (birth or chosen) dies, you may need to devise your own rites; or you may feel too devastated to begin. This is a suggestion.

Preparation

For this ritual, you will need a box with a lid (something about the size that holds computer paper is a good size), some gifts for children between the ages of birth and legal majority, cheerful wrapping paper, dirt, flowers, a tray or something else to hold the lidded box, a piece of black cloth big enough to cover the box, and a candle. The gifts should be things that you would have expected one day to give to the child who has died. Do not make these things symbolic. Buy or make real gifts: stuffed animals, key chains, books, dolls, toy cars, sets of stationery, and yes, even underwear.

[9]From "Farewell, I Bid You (on Your Way to Summerland)," first printed in *The Family Wicca Book* (Llewellyn, 1993).

The Ritual

In Circle, wrap these gifts in cheerful paper, and talk as much as you can about what you hoped it would be like to give these things to the child you're mourning. Acknowledge the occasions you'll miss sharing with this child. Share your dashed hopes. Cry together. Pound your fists on the ground if you feel like it, sob; let your tears fall on the wrapping paper.

When the gifts are wrapped, put them in the box and set the cover on it. Sprinkle some dirt over the top of the box. Lay your flowers over the top, just like you would (or did) on the coffin. When you are ready, drape the black cloth over the box, covering even the flowers.

Toast the departed soul with "Cakes and Ale" (cookies and milk?). Peace, freedom and reunion. Pass the cup around between each word of the toast, or at the end, according to your preference under the circumstances.

When that is done, light a candle in front of the black-draped box and say, "By the life that is eternal, we pledge to honor the energy this child _____ raised with us in the Circle of Life, and ever to honor the smallest steps around the Wheel."

Let this candle burn down; if you need to, move it to assure that it is safe and undisturbed. When the candle has burned out, *then* fold the black cloth. Save it to use for other ritual or as a ground for gazing crystals, make pouches of it, or find some other way to recycle its energy. Do what you will with the dirt and flowers. Pressing and saving the flowers is nice if you keep scrapbooks; they will also be powerful in charms, or meaningful as compost. Then put the box of gifts by until Yule.

At Yule, before you get around to the usual festivities, get the box down. Take it to the fire station or the TV station or wherever in your community gifts for needy children are collected. On a holiday gift card write, "In memory of

_____, in celebration of [the Sun's] rebirth." If you're stuck "in the broom closet," tuck that tag in down at the bottom; no one will know that *you* left it, but *do* use the tag. It will help, and once this is done, you'll be able to enjoy the holiday at least a little bit knowing that you have honored your child's spirit in other children's lives.

Another way of dealing with death is through myth. This is not likely to be an immediate response, although if you are accustomed to "living mythically," you may be able to take up the various duties surrounding death with an adventurous attitude. And once the immediate obligations are met, almost all of us begin to "mythify" our loved ones.

Whether we type them as tyrants or heroes depends on our relationships. But it is quite natural, and I think healthy, to reaffirm a dead person's significance to and continuing influence on the community and the individual lives therein. A few years ago, a woman who was already half-legendary among us here in Tucson died. Here is the story I wrote about her, which was published in our network's newsletter.[10]

One of the Children's Favorite Stories

"Tell me again about the First Grandmother," the child asked eagerly. We had been telling the Old Stories all afternoon; I'd been waiting for the child to ask for this one.

"A very long time ago," I began, softening the words toward a whisper, "before the First Day of Time, lived the First Grandmother, and she danced like shadows and sun." I paused. The child and I closed our eyes and watched the First Grandmother dance.

[10]In respectful memory of Shona Jackson, High Priestess, Elder, Sister, Dawn Singer, Shaman, Guide; Goddess. Reprinted from *Tapestry*, the Tucson Area Wiccan Network's newsletter, Ostara, 1990 C.E.

"And then she danced with her feet, and then she danced with her hands, and then she danced with her songs, and then she danced with her heart," I told, and the child's lips moved with mine.

"The First Grandmother first appeared to our people as a Queen, robed in silver music, sounding the rhythm of life with every step."

The child bounced at my feet and blurted out the next few lines. "And her hair was long and black and silver like the threads of the Cosmos; and with her walked her attendants, Shadow and Power." I had not known the child had learned so much of the story. I smiled.

"The First Grandmother was a High Priestess to our people, and she was a shaman among us, and she lived among our people for some time. And while she was among us, our people were enriched.

"And the First Grandmother undertook many hardships and many dangerous adventures, and our people marveled at her courage and felt awe when they felt her spirit.

"The First Grandmother made gifts to our people, gifts of beauty and wisdom. She gave them her runes; and when our people looked up from these gifts, they saw that the First Grandmother stood no longer before them."

"Why did she leave them?" the child wondered aloud for both of us.

"She did not *leave* our people," I proclaimed formally, and the child's lips moved with mine again. "She changed her aspect to us. Our people knew this, too, for they could still feel her among them, as *we* do, and as *your* children's children will."

"And when you make her silver music," the child said, holding two pendants up so they rang together, "you think of her and remember the dance."

"Ah, child," I sighed, "I wish you could remember the dancer as well."

"It's alright, Gran'," the child reminded me. "I *do* remember her, from every time you tell me; and I *hear* her." The pendants chimed again, and I heard her, too.

Then the child's expression became innocently sly. "Give me your bracelets, Gran', and let me wear your straw hat with the strings, and I can *be* the dancer."

And I could see that it was true, for the child's eyes were already dancing like the First Grandmother's.

In my community, there has been some discussion about the practice of having the body present at a memorial service or funeral. It is important that at least some people in the family or coven or community see the dead body; otherwise, psychologically, it can be difficult to accept that the body has, indeed, died.

For this reason, I have always liked the idea of an open casket at the service. But many Witches in my community find this distasteful, and object as well to the artificiality and additional expense of embalming. I don't share the esthetic objections, but I respect them, and I do share the financial objections! Discussion and private thought on such issues can lead us to creative resolutions that meet everybody's needs without compromising principles. While I was taking a daydreaming break from writing this book, I had an idea that could work for some of us: make a death mask.

It came to mind when my unfocused gaze came to rest on the Green Man that hangs sometimes in our kitchen: a glittery face mask from a craft store, decorated with silk leaves and pine cones. I think a death mask is a great idea; and you can even make one now, if you like. Death masks can be decorated and used in rituals other than requiems, too. One might later be used as an offering bowl, or even as a candle-shield. Framed, it might hang on the wall as a portrait, and no doubt there are other ways to use such a piece for group or personal ritual. Death masks are traditional in many cultures—including Wicca's Anglo-Celtic ancestry—and *very* powerful tools. (How do you make one? Ask your librarian. Call it a life mask, if you need to; make a life mask now, if the idea of making a death mask later makes you squeamish.)

Ashes can be scattered at a particular site annually, they can be mixed with anointing oil—they can even be baked into special cakes and eaten in Circle, something vaguely reminiscent of what we believe our ancestors to have done to celebrate death. Ashes were once, and I believe still are in some communities, communally shared in cakes or ale. As an act of sympathetic magic affirming rebirth, this is very powerful magic. (Some people wonder whether this is cannibalistic. Eating flesh is. Tasting ashes isn't.) We can make, of a pinch of a loved one's ashes, a cake or cup for the Gods, of which we do not partake ourselves but offer as libation to symbolize the departed soul's belonging in the God/dess' Circle. You could "make a cup" more literally and fire ashes into a clay chalice, too.

As you find time and courage to explore these ideas and the ideas *you* will have, you'll find death presenting itself more beautifully to you. You'll feel the power of death, and you'll feel your life charged with that power.

You've seen the almost painfully beautiful portrait of the Earth from space. From the perspective of death as a part of life, a patch of sunlight on the carpet, ephemeral as it is, can evoke the same sense of awe. In remembering our dead we are no more limited in the rituals we devise than the Goddess is limited in Her expressions of life. Like Her, may we remember that there is never a farewell without a welcome.

PART TWO

Whenever someone or something dies, there are details to attend to. There are legalities and matters of protocol; there are decisions to be made and tissues to be passed around and people to explain it to when they call and don't know.

In Part Two we'll look at some of the very practical requirements that death sets for us, the arrangements and decisions that need to be made. The very strong feelings that we have about death are raw energies, and we'll talk about some of the ways we can direct those energies constructively.

For Wiccans, the God is all that dies and is reborn. It is the God we follow when we ourselves die, or when part of us—a dear companion, a life-long hope, even a sense of direction—dies. (He is not only the game that's hunted and the grain that's harvested for our clans' Winter survival, and He is not only you and me. He is also our hopes and dreams, our missed opportunities and our aging accomplishments.) In His attitudes we find examples of the magic we can do with the creativity and courage that is Life's birthright. In His actions and the stages of His life we find models for our own.

Death has nearly as many faces as Life has, and so Part Two talks about a wide range of circumstances in which we encounter death. There is some more thealogy here, amongst the musings and considerations of Wicca's ethics. Part Two is challenging, and conjures the Guardians a little, looking at clinical, social and psychological realities in some depth. More important than how deeply we go into any point, though, is the need to plumb the depths at all. Part Two gives some specific examples of the mundane details of death, redescribing them in Wiccan terms.

When we are most stressed, we are most dependent on the nurture of our infancies and early childhoods. If we learned love and trust when we were babies, we can bring that confidence to any crisis and it will help us to ground and center. A good many of us, though, came up under child-rearing theories that were expressed as "spare the rod, spoil the child," or "children should be seen and not heard," or "oh, no, dear, you don't feel *that* way," or worse. Perhaps you remember. A lot of us have recovered from those theories, mostly, but we're still at risk of falling back on them when we're really low.

A lot of those child-rearing theories were pretty threatening, and in such systems of belief, the ultimate threat is death. So to fall back on how we were treated when we were tiny is to fall back on insecurity at best, fear at worst. But death for Wiccans is *not* a threat. It's a Gate on a Path. It's a step in the process, a step in the Dance. The love of the God/dess is unconditional, S/he is us; and collectively with everything else, we are the Gods. When we recognize Him as a hero for His forays through mortality, we can recognize ourselves as heroic too.

Death is an honor, an adventure requiring great skill and courage—and we are by nature equal to it. Fully human, I believe, we are Gods; because of this innate personalization, the Wheel of the Year is a global calendar. Part Two grounds us and reminds us how to use our energy to turn the Wheel—even, and especially, for ourselves.

Death and the God

The Wiccan calendar follows the annual life of "all that dies and is reborn," which we call the God. The Wheel of the Year marks His birth, His growing, His maturity, His dying. *We* die too; and if He is reborn, *we* must be reborn as well. This is why we celebrate His death in the service of life: we are absolutely certain that He will be reborn and grow again to provision the future's harvests and hunts.

It is His death which makes His rebirth possible—"for to be born, you must die"—and it's by all of His examples in the world that we know our deaths will make our rebirths possible, too. The God dies in the harvest that will fill the granaries and replant the fields that He will make green again come Spring. He dies to the arrow after the rut, so that the clan will have meat and warm furs for the winter. Sprouting from the fields and reborn from the ewes and cows, He will grow and gambol again come Spring. So too our lives nourish the world when we die, and so too are we reborn.

In every Wiccan Sabbat, there is an awareness of its twin. At the Summer's Solstice, when the Sun is high and strong, we know that at Yule it will be low and faint. Yet we celebrate the fading of the Sun as well. At Yule when some might call it old and feeble, looking toward Litha's brilliance, we call the Sun newborn. We know that the old Sun becomes the new Sun, and we celebrate the knowing (trust) as well as the becoming (love). And at the same time, there is another twin knowledge: death is a becoming, too.

We know our God, and this is His way, His nature. He does not fear death; and He is our guide so that we need not fear it either. Our God does not cry out or feel forsaken when He falls, for He knows that He returns, and He longs to return, to the Mother. And He knows that from Her, He will be reborn. We can know that, too.

When we ask, *"Why do people have to die?"* we usually mean why did _____ have to die? For each individual, of course, there's a different answer. But the bottom line is that people—and all other things—die because we're mortal. Come into being, live, and die is what mortal things do. It's our job. It's a cycle: the Sun and Moon rise and set and wax and wane, the seasons turn, the oceans rise and fall. People have to die because to be reborn you have to die, and we want to be reborn because Wholeness longs for Individuality as much as Individuality longs for Wholeness.

The late Elisabeth Kübler-Ross did amazing and fundamental research into the emotional aspects of dying. In her watershed *On Death and Dying*,[1] she identified five emotions people have to confront when they're dying, if they haven't done so earlier. Her advocacy was for the patient's present moment, and her advice to us all is to live in the present moment, emotionally.

We need to remember that the creative expression of strong emotions (which could easily be destructive) is a Witch's business. Strong emotions are energy, and energy is what we "bend and shape." We can consider our feelings among our *tools*, and realize that knowing and being able to work with our emotions is just as important as knowing and being able to work with our athames or wands or cords.

Let's look at the feelings that Kübler-Ross calls "stages" of death. One is denial and isolation. Sounds a *lot* like, "No, really, really, it wasn't me, I didn't do that, I wasn't even here when it

---

[1]Elisabeth Kübler-Ross, *On Death and Dying* (Collier Books, MacMillan Publishing Co., New York, 1969).

happened!" and "Go to your room and stay there!" Which in turn might have been what went on next door last week, or in the Garden of Eden. Wiccan thealogy presents death as heroic and healing, something to be expected and prepared for with reverence, an act, like many others in our lives, which we may accomplish well or poorly. To the extent that any physical capacity or ability can be a tool, dying is a tool for us to use once, at the end of our lives.

This is not to say that Wiccans won't or shouldn't say "No! No! This cannot be!" But death of the body not only can but *must* happen. Fear doesn't have to. We cannot successfully (or reverently) deny the death of our bodies, but we can successfully deny guilt and fear. The energy we raise through denial can be constructively directed to reinforce our fearlessness. If we look at the Celtic myths that are part of Wicca's heritage, we find many heroic and magical images to inspire us. Writing our own deathing rituals, acting out myths that encourage us and "resonate" within us, strengthens us and our communities.

Another stage people commonly go through is anger. Wicca attaches no moral sanctions to anger, and the only duty toward it we have is the Rede- and Law-derived responsibility to direct it creatively. Certainly there is no prohibition against *raising* the energy of anger, and like the energy of denial, anger's energy can be redirected. In the mythical contexts of Pagan religions, these energies can be finessing, too, putting a unique personal "spin" on our own death, and so on our community's understanding of death, the universe, and everything.

Bargaining is one more stage of grief the dying and the bereaved may go through. It's not just the B-movie promise to do 597 billion Hail Marys if only God will let you live. It's also the idea that if you submit to certain medical care, you'll be healed, or if you're nicer to people you don't like or otherwise follow the rules more successfully, none of this might really have to happen. Or not, at least, until somebody graduates or gets married, or till

the book's finished. There is no presumed doom in Wicca's thealogy, so Wiccans' bargaining need not be frantic or desperate. This
last burst of interest in control over the mortal coil can be a push
of effort to weave up all the loose ends, or an inspiration to charge
survivors, or both, or more.

Depression sometimes comes to people who have been told or
feel that death is imminent, and it often comes to people who
have survived a loved one's death. It's a combination of feelings,
including confusion, anxiety, and disorientation as well as desperate unhappiness. Depression is also a symptom of transitions. The
rules are changing, expectations are changing, the changes are both
gross and subtle. They are dramatic changes, yet not necessarily
obvious. When you don't know the rules, you don't know how to
act . . . or how to feel.

The emptiness that depression feels like can, however, be filled.
You may not be able to "talk" a dying friend out of her depression, but you may be able to facilitate a ritual that will empower
her to bring herself out of it. In ritual or in earnest conversation
you can encourage anyone who's dying to accept responsibility
for the control s/he still has. In earnest conversation and in meditation, you can encourage yourself to die well, too.

To the extent that depression is an organic syndrome, we are
bound to feel it now and again. Depression turns our attention
inward. Consider the effect this might have had in ancient societies. Understand it as serving evolution: depression could be in
the service of life. However, when depression (and it takes many
forms) lasts longer than six months, or interferes with your life, see
a doctor. Depression can feel like a form of death, and there are
medications that will "give you back your life." It is not wrong,
unnatural, or disrespectful to get treatment for it. Nor, for dying
patients, is the treatment of depression a waste of time. (The truth
is, while suffering can be instructive, you can also exhaust the use
of suffering. Some religions value suffering for its own sake. Wicca
doesn't.)

In grief, we are hyper-needy of our clan's support, both physically and psychically. Depression inhibits our motivation, leaving us temporarily disinterested in the Quest, yet still receptive. In that way, depression is a healthy withdrawal, excusing us from ordinary work, yet leaving us receptive to the ministrations of our kinfolk. It's my speculation and meditation that in the Old Days,[2] depression functioned as a biochemical Gate to the Underworld, through which mourners could take a parallel journey to the dead person's. With the loving support of the rest of the clan (using the term loosely), the most bereaved could follow their loved one some distance into the Realms Beyond.

I wonder if the multicultural tradition of tearing one's garments when a family member dies is not a fragment of an ancient re-enactment of a story similar to the one Wiccans tell of the Goddess's Descent. The Goddess does not die, but She experiences death in another way, just as when someone we love dies, *we* experience death in a different way. The Goddess, eternal though She is, could make the Descent; so can we share that much of the experience with our loved ones.

Wearing black (so that one's role as a mourner overshadows one's individuality), seclusion and withdrawing from social interplay for a period of time, and other such cultural acknowledgments of death may be remnants of once-powerful journeying rituals. An expanded participation in a beloved's death could be of comfort to the bereaved, and it would reinforce the tribal interpretation of the process.

I think that Witches can make particularly wonderful use of the depression that can set in over death. A well-prepared Priest/ess could work with a mourner's or a dying friend's depression and provide an opportunity for its transformation. Days of drumming, maybe; chanting, hours on end. We find it noble and holistic to have midwives on call and we are prepared (quite a few of us,

---

[2]Prehistorically, say, 60,000 to 7500 B.C.E.

anyway) to dash off for several hours to a home-birth at a moment's notice. Shall we give less attention to death? We hope that once it is clear that death is close, we will be able to take an attitude of acceptance, another stage of reaction that Kübler-Ross identified, but we don't need to confuse acceptance with eagerness.

Oh, but what if you *don't* feel "the way you're supposed to" feel? Feelings are pretty personal, and yours are your business. The only thing of public concern is what you do, how you act (in all the realms, though, I think) as a consequence of your feelings. It's easier to cope with feelings, experience tells us, if we can share them with friends. Some people can share their feelings with apparent ease, but it's not easy for everybody.

When our feelings are new or unpleasant or frighteningly intense, it's easy to think that nobody else has ever felt the same way. When we're out of control or out of line, we worry that other people will condemn us or reject us. We don't want to confront that fear because even though hiding our feelings isolates us, we're afraid that sharing them might end up isolating us even more. We risk falling into an abyss of anxiety, self-doubt, and paranoia, and it's destructive; the good news is that you can bet your mortgage that what you're feeling, so have other people, and so *do* other people, and so *will* other people, because "we are the same people," as the chant reminds us.

Keep in mind that no matter how any of us feel, most of our feelings fall within the "normal" range of human experience. Sadness, with all its component feelings, is a natural reaction to loss, and no matter what wonders are in store for us when we die, parting with those we love here and now *is* sad. But people feel and express sadness in different ways: some people cry, some people rage, some people don't feel like smiling for a while. (Most of us react in a variety of ways.)

Some people need to be reminded and encouraged to eat and sleep and stay healthy while they grieve. Others seem not to grieve at all. Barring psychotic chemical imbalance, people who don't *display* their grief still *feel* it when a loved one dies—or when they learn that they themselves are soon to die. You can trust a healthy body and brain to respond with "normal" human feelings to death; by nature's standards, what you *do* feel is what you're supposed to feel.

It would be a bad sign if our awareness of our own mortality wasn't heightened by other deaths; that's why it bothers us how many violent deaths we can see on television, and why we worry about being desensitized. If someone you know dies doing something you do—driving a car, climbing a mountain, having an illness—it's natural to wonder, even fleetingly, whether the same thing might not happen to you. The winter he had pneumonia, the Explorer suffered through one long, lonely night before he confided in us that he thought he was going to die because (a completely different type of) pneumonia had taken Muppeteer Jim Henson's life a few months earlier.

And it's natural to be angry *at* someone who has died, especially when they've died suddenly. It feels *as if* that person copped out on your relationship when there were issues left hanging, projects unfinished. By the time the two of you meet again, you'll both have forgotten any unresolved arguments or unfulfilled promises; but in the meantime, anger, frustration, and annoyance are all perfectly natural. Indeed, those strong, aggressive feelings generate the body chemistry, like adrenaline, that keeps us going through the critical few days following someone's death, when everything that has to be done is difficult.

Legal matters attend everything like bees after honey. People have to be told, funeral arrangements made, closets and attics and rooms gone through and Things disposed of, letters have to be written—Decisions have to be made. There's enough work to sap ten people on a good day, and it usually falls to one person. We evolved the response of anger; death-tasks can channel anger's "fight energy" and turn "flight" energy to reassurance. On the other hand, it's not un-normal to decide that those unresolved issues aren't worth being bothered about now that you've been through stuff that's *really* important. While her husband was in the hospital, my friend said that one of the doctors gave her some advice: "There are two rules," he told her. "First, don't sweat the small stuff; second, it's all small stuff."

Dying people, when they know what's going on, are often angry at having to end their lives. We help them best when we encourage them to be specific about that anger. Sometimes the explorations and complaints come to nothing more than the peace of release and acknowledgment; sometimes we discover a way to complete a life, at least symbolically, before it leaves the physical plane. In either case, it can be hard to hear these angers enumerated. It's hard to see other people cry—but easier if you remember that it's alright to cry *with* them. And if you can't think of anything to say, that's alright, too, because nobody's really asking you to *say* anything. Really, most times it's enough if you just don't go away.

Sometimes the anger is ours. Sometimes death is not, at least not obviously, in the service of life. It is up to us to *make* sense of senseless deaths, to find or *make* the way in which a "senseless" death will serve life. When we look for the meaning in somebody else's life and death, we change our own lives. Change is an opportunity for growth. Growth is life. If we grow on the energy someone's death has raised in us, then that person "lives" in our growth. Growth is life, and that's one way a senseless death can be made sense of and brought into the service of life.

The God's death is "in the service of life," a nourishing act. Any natural death is in the service of life, for naturally death is a return to the Mother's womb. Any natural death is in the service of life; what about "unnatural" death? No, not the kind where the slime crabs from outer space grab you on your way up that seldom-used path through the woods, but accidental deaths, inexplicable deaths, murders, that sort of thing. What about *those*?

My dear friend's husband's death was like that, inexplicable at first and apparently meaningless. She did not accept one chaplain's assertion that this death was "God's will" or that it was "all for the good," a part of some plan. Although some Christian clergy believe it, Wiccan thealogy does not support the idea that Grianwydd's husband (or anyone else) had to die so that some other part of The Divine Plan could go forward. That's zero-sum thinking in clerical frocks.

Avalon's death occurred, releasing energy, and Grianwydd's direction of that energy, her "priestessing" of that energy as a shepherd guides the flock through the valley, clarified her sense of the meaning of his life. The ways she found to ground the energy released in his death, and the process she went through in deciding how to ground that energy, contributed to the meaning of his life, too. (As it happens, the experience called her to Presbyterian ordination, and everyone who knows her is enormously proud of her effort and courage.)

Remember that anger is *energy*. If you are a Witch, you know (or should!) something about directing energy. You know something about transforming energy, too, and maybe you can share that with someone who is dying. Maybe you can help a friend to release her anger in atonal chanting, which can be transformed to something that reinfuses her with peace or joy. Sorrow and fear can be released and transformed in this way, too.

Imagine a darkened hospital room, candles (not always permitted—consider electrics) flickering on the counter, the figure in the bed surrounded by a circle of gently swaying figures whose entranced faces shine with love. They are triple chanting: "We all come from the Goddess" and "Isis, Astarte" and "Goddess is alive, magic is afoot," and the power is as thick as incense. The death is peaceful, and when the Priestess perceives it, she turns the chant and it becomes "Jubilate Gaia"[3] and fills the room with the same light that beckons their departing friend. They step aside for the

---

[3] This exquisitely beautiful round was first sung for me by Nancy K. and Deb R., and as far as I know, Nancy created it from some traditional music and her own love of singing and Goddess. It is still part of our community's choral repertoire.

medical team, who understand what is happening and leave the body for a while. The people sing for half an hour, and then each of them takes a watch beside the body, encouraging the soul to speed toward the Goddess.

These people are sad when they leave the hospital, and tired, and they miss their friend. Yet the helplessness (a major source of anger in life-and-death situations) they felt when they first heard of her illness was displaced by their purposeful gathering at the death-bed. Their anger was transformed to support of their dying friend because the covenant of participation was not broken in the end. They can feel a little like midwives, and keep their focus on life.

Remembering that anger is energy, and that dealing with energy is our stock in trade, it can be relatively easy for Wiccan clergy to deal with the anger dying people raise, and with the anger survivors feel on behalf of the dying. We don't have any moral prohibitions against anger, and we do have lots of ritual ways to acknowledge and ground it. That there might be any good come from the anger we sometimes feel *toward* someone who's died is more difficult to accept.

Anger's energy is not to be wasted on things that don't matter. Anger—if it is at least carefully and at best ritually released and not taken out violently in the world—can be bonding, can be an invocation of the warts-and-all humanity of someone you love, a way of appreciating the magnitude of the loss, the fragile beauty of life, and all the rest of those fundamentals that make us cry in longing. It's also true that hiding our feelings from someone we're close enough to go through death with is taxing and unfair. We sometimes think to shield the dying from unpleasantness, but while people are alive, we should treat them that way with our whole selves.

Of course, people who don't harbor much anger, people who acknowledge frustrations and deal creatively with them, solving problems instead of scoring points off them, may not feel anger toward people for dying. If there weren't any issues outstanding, there might not be much to get mad about. Maybe the extra housework. What about anger on *behalf* of someone who has died, anger at the lost years, anger and frustration and disappointment? That's real normal too. I can still come to fury about my friend's husband's death (it's been more than 10 years now), and I was angry for 'dancer when he wrecked his back, losing strength and agility. (He has since regained them. I was angry on his behalf when he had a heart attack, too, from which he has, thank God/dess, completely recovered.)

But when the anger has been resolved—some people deny themselves resolution, of course, mistaking it for a luxury and thinking they don't deserve it—one is free to grieve honestly. We can remember the dead as real people and instead of feeling guilty for noticing their imperfections, we can begin to find in their ordinary lives (and by extension, in ours) the elements of heroic adventure.

Something else we may feel when someone dies is relief. If a loved one is lingering, unconscious, tubed and wired or otherwise deprived of the capacity to participate in his own life, death can be the proverbial blessing. If the loss has already been felt and the only future is attendance upon (and imprisonment within) a help-less husk, then death is welcomed, and relief is appropriate.

Acceptance is characterized by a certain realism, by a subtle acknowledgment that it's time to get the harvest in and a subtle decision to do that work with as much style and dignity as you can. Now, we all have different ideas of an ideal death; if you're not really familiar with yours, *get* familiar with it. There is no question but what you will die; the only questions are details, and the most important one is with what *attitude*?[4]

There are many in the world who don't know that we can be in control of our attitudes. Society is happy to dictate to us how

[4]Einstein, I heard or read somewhere, maintained that the only important question is, "Is the Universe friendly?" and from his deathbed he is said to have declared that the answer to that question is yes. Now *that's* a good attitude!

we should feel and how we should approach the events of our lives. But the God's example for us is to know our own feelings. Death in the service of life must for us be a conscious choice, and we can only make choices from freedom; freedom is *really having* significant choices. As long as we're unfamiliar or uncomfortable with our feelings and values and attitudes, or shamed by or for them, or unable to articulate and express them, we're not free.

I would say that changing an attitude is one of the most basic sorts of magic there is. "Magic is the art of changing consciousness at will," Dion Fortune said. Starhawk calls magic "the art of sensing and shaping the subtle." Scott Cunningham said that "Magic is the projection of natural energies to produce needed effects." Crowley called magic "the Science and Art of causing Change to occur in conformity with Will." Nothing in any of those definitions precludes us turning that magic on ourselves to establish the attitudes we choose to have. Indeed, personal growth is the real aim of most magic. So we are *not* stuck with conventional attitudes and feelings toward death; neither are we without alternatives to conventional behaviors.

The conventional public image of the Wiccan God is Pan-like, grown, skilled, lusty, and a mate in all senses of the word. But the God is not only our Lady's consort, He is her *Son*, and when He dies, She loses a child as well as a lover. It's not something we like to hang pictures of in the living room (anymore), but death is part of children's lives too.

There are a lot of ways to talk to children about death, help them understand it; there is nothing you can say to lessen the grief of those who mourn a child. It's a good idea to talk to kids, before you "need" to, about death. It's unrealistic to intend to lessen anyone's grief when a child dies.

No matter how you end up feeling about it once you've worked through it, there is no escape from feeling rotten and horrible when it happens or almost happens. *Go* with these feelings, plunge into them and brave the full experience. Not because we're here to suffer in the first place, but because plunging right in is such an appropriate mirror of and tribute to a kid's life. Kids live in the moment, and most of them live through it; so can we.

We cannot protect each other or ourselves from grief. It is a biochemical imperative; but we can steady each other through it. "Exposing" children to death as a part of life robs them of no innocence: it is innocent to accept death as part of life. *Fear* is the corruption. Denying death to children (and euphemizing or abstracting their own deaths) inspires that fear. (It's also true that acknowledging death can freak the bejeebers out of children, so we have to be careful how much we tell them and in what terms and contexts. For example, about six months after the event, a documentary about "9-11" that included new ground-zero footage was aired with a warning that it might traumatize children, and some adults, all over again.)

Surviving Other Losses

Death, pennies-over-the-eyelids death, is not the only loss we suffer; nor is it the only one to which our brain chemistry responds. Other losses or loss-like stresses—a lover's parting, the threat of job loss, family vendettas, scary neighbors, serious chronic illnesses—can feel like a lot like death to us.

Whenever we feel like we've lost something or someone important to us, we go through the stages of grief in some degree. It's perfectly normal to deny, to be depressed, to bargain, and to feel some anger before we finally accept a loss; and sometimes we *don't* accept it.

Most of us have said to ourselves, at one time or another, "I've got to pull myself together and get *over* this!" Do you? And if you do, how? Well, yes, you probably *do* have to "pull yourself together" eventually, and that's a good way of putting it, too. But you might not have to pull yourself together immediately, and you *absolutely* don't have to do it by disowning your feelings.

A lot of us like to say that "nothing happens but for a reason." This doesn't mean there's any external force directing us like some giant six-year-old playing figures with our lives. It means that we have both the capacity and the inclination, and maybe an obligation as well, to see meaning in the events of our lives. It's like, now that you know how to read, it's very difficult *not* to read when you see letters.

When something rotten happens, when you suffer a loss, you don't have to believe that the bad thing happened in *order that* something else (good) could happen. Looking at it that way, it would be easy to feel that enjoying any good fortune that followed upon a loss was like taking dirty money. That premise also makes it easy to think that if something good happens, or if things are going well, something bad is bound to happen. "No good deed goes unpunished," we joke. Bad joke. Really, when bad things—no, let's call them *unexpected* things—when *unexpected* things happen, it's perfectly alright to see where you can go from where they leave you. It's not a betrayal of anybody or anything to pick yourself up, dust yourself off, and get on with your life.

In the Adventure Tradition, we put a lot of emphasis on camaraderie, even between lovers. On the few occasions that we've been faced with life-threatening situations, we've found it helpful. When you're on an adventure and one of your number falls, you honor that comrade to the fullest extent circumstances will allow (sometimes it can't be properly done till later), and then you carry on with the Quest.

You don't feel guilty about carrying on, either, because after all, your fallen companion was dedicated to the same Quest—Life, putting it very generally—and died in its service. Abandoning the Quest doesn't make much sense in that light. No, the Right Thing To Do is to carry on, and with as much heart and gusto as you can, too. In that way, you honor not only your companion's memory in the world, affirming the communal value of what mattered to that person, but you also honor your relationship by affirming the importance of your experience in common.

Now, this is fairly easy to understand in terms of someone dying, but it's more difficult to translate in practical terms when the loss is of another kind. Not every loss is so well-defined or radical as death, but the less finite losses can give us just as much trouble.

When my friend's husband went into a coma early one summer a decade or so ago, nobody knew why at first. (Eventually they realized it was a complication of his diabetes.) Nobody knew how long he would be like that, either. He wasn't on life support systems, except for the feeding tube. He was a little responsive, not even close to brain dead. There were no choices for my friend and the medical team. All they could do was wait, and this they did bravely and graciously.

But my friend is a vital woman. She is ordinarily vibrant, attentive and game for 'most anything. She is a striking woman, too, somebody you'd notice right away without feeling intruded upon; yet under the very difficult circumstances of her husband's illness, she nearly disappeared.

Disappeared? Yes, and it happens to lots of other people, too. Whenever there is a life-threatening emergency, the resources of any community—whether it's the nuclear family, the coven, the bowling buddies or the hospital—focus tightly on whoever's sick, no matter what else is happening. So my friend, like tens of thousands of other spouses and children and mothers and fathers and sisters and brothers of chronically ill people, nearly disappeared because *she* was healthy, *she* was alright, *she* could take care of herself, *she* didn't need anything.

Oh, yeah? Well, *no*. That's exactly wrong. I saw her routine. Every day she made the 10- or 20-minute drive to the hospital, checked in with the doctors and nurses on duty, checked in with the families of other patients who'd been in Intensive Care at the same time, and then went to her husband's bedside. She read him the paper, caught him up on the gossip, told him what the dogs had done lately, and reassured him that she loved him. She stroked him, moved his arms about, encouraged him to turn his head or follow her with his eyes—even though they said that was mostly a sort of limbic response, almost reflexive, and only *maybe* conscious communication.

When people called to talk to her on the phone or leave messages on her machine, they'd ask how her husband was, not how she was doing. People told her how much she must be looking forward to his recovery, without realizing that the medical reality was that, yes, he *might* regain consciousness, but probably *not* in terms of full function. In other words, people expected her to be thrilled at the prospect of being committed to the gracious care of a brain-damaged invalid for the rest of her life—or at least for the rest of his, which could have been another 30 or 40 years. Would *you* be thrilled?

Mainstay[1] was the name of the book she asked me to read, and I read it, and then I read it again for the parts I couldn't see through the tears the first time. The loneliness and insecurity we can feel when subtle losses consume our lives is quite awesome, even overwhelming, at least sometimes. It is in these circumstances, I think, that Kübler-Ross's five stages of grief show up most clearly. Unfortunately, I think it is under these circumstances that these emotional landscapes seem most hostile. Whether the loss is of a relationship or a lifestyle or a job or a dream, it's hard to adjust, and harder still when it's not acknowledged as *your* loss.

Kids go through it when their parents get divorced. Employees go through it when their bosses talk about retirement or think about mid-life career changes. Husbands and wives go through it in many ways. Parents go through it when children grow up and lay hold of their independence. Your pets have to deal with it when the family moves. You face it when something rotten happens to a really good friend.

All these situations—examples, really, as this is certainly not a comprehensive list—affect people in varying degrees and with different mitigations. These are the sorts of things that bring people to personal brinks. The conventional response tends to be, "It's God's will; get used to it." (Sometimes it's worse than that: sometimes there's an attendant guilt trip for your temerity in worrying about yourself at a time like this.)

---

[1] Maggie Strong, *Mainstay: for the Well Spouse of the Chronically Ill* (Penguin Books, New York, 1988). An endorsement on the front cover says, "If you are married to a chronically ill person, read *Mainstay* . . . *Whatever* you feel, you are not alone." It's a must-read if you Circle with or in any way minister to or are otherwise very close to anybody chronically ill, or even if you ever might be.

Another sort of loss many of us have to face is chronic (and maybe progressive) disability. Canyondancer's disability requires him to lie down for at least a couple of hours every day, and it limits the sorts of things he can do around the house, in the yard and when we're camping; some things he's had to learn how to do differently. We don't face a progressive deterioration of his condition, but when he was first hurt, we didn't know that.

We know Witches who are confined to wheelchairs, and whose conditions are worsening. For such Witches, there are the usual problems of accessibility, something that the Craft has been addressing of late. We've had a Witch help us braid the Maypole from her motorized wheelchair, so we know that access-to-ritual problems aren't insoluble. Accessibility to an attitude of power may be a stickier wicket, though. Our fellow Wiccans can help us maneuver and design accessible rites; does Wicca itself have anything to offer us if we're handicapped?[2]

That I know of, there is nothing in any of Wicca's liturgical material commanding us to be physically perfect or implying that our power is reduced by physical handicap. (Yes, there's that old bugaboo about an "imperfect" king being unfit to rule; but in a lot of those stories, a prosthesis—Celtic mythology's Nuada's silver hand leaps to mind—is restorative.) What most Wiccan teaching holds is that our Power is diminished only by our own foibles and follies, and the way we handle our energy is still within our control even when we suffer physical impairments.

Pain, of course, is distracting. Conventional medical science has begun to realize that there are "treatments" for pain that don't involve mind-dulling drugs: biofeedback is increasingly popular in

[2] I mean no disrespect by using this term. None of the so-called politically correct terms are as clear, it seems to me, as *handicapped*, although it would sure be nice if physically disabled people got the same sort of benefit from their handicaps as, say, golfers do. Instead of starting with compensating advantages, though, most handicapped people find themselves *further* handicapped by people's attitudes. We hope that using the term *handicapped* here to refer to any and all physical problems that limit and impair us, temporarily or permanently, life-threateningly or not, will not be misunderstood as any prejudice.

rehabilitation programs, and ancient treatments like acupuncture and acupressure are also beginning to find acceptance even in conservative medical communities; plain ol' exercise and social contact can help, too.

Many of these "alternative" treatments are compatible with Wicca, and supportable in Circle and in magical work generally. Although the people you gather with for Moons and Sabbats may not be medically trained, if they are magically trained they can help you bring the energy of chronic pain back under your own control through breathing and other yogic exercises, and by offering support in biofeedback techniques. Grounding and centering can help a lot, as can "running the chakras," which is to say, coordinating breathing and awareness to open the psychic and naturally healing centers of your own body.

For many years *mirth* has been a useful tool in fighting some diseases: working in a law office specializing in disability, I've seen Laurel and Hardy prescribed for depression, and now visualization techniques are gaining wider acceptance, too. We have probably all read or seen discussions of people who put their own cancers in remission through visualizations that combined images of their bodies' workings with "the will to live" to create confident visions of recovery. Personally, I'm hard put to draw the line between this sort of visualization and a magical spell.

But thealogically, does Wicca offer any consolation, or maybe more to the point, any *explanation*, to people who wonder, *Why me?* Well, very generally, of course, to be reborn you must die; also very generally, the Goddess requires naught of sacrifice, which in my mind translates to the idea that death isn't a sacrifice as we commonly use the term. Doors do not close without other ones opening. So while I must admit that I don't think Wicca is terribly sympathetic in the *awww, poor baby* sense, I assert that Wicca offers us something of more value than pity, which is expectation.

It's said that blind people can achieve almost miraculous development of the physical senses remaining to them; likewise, I think that any given disadvantage may suggest the greater development of other facilities or opportunities. Rebirth isn't just about the death of the body and the soul's subsequent reincarnation in another one. Rebirth, as we know from our experience of Initiation, can also comprise a refocusing of our attention on qualities and characteristics we might otherwise neglect. I think this is a great lesson of Wicca: thou art God/dess; i.e., there must be something wonderful and holy about you.

It's easy to recognize what's wonderful about a gold-medal athlete or a graceful dancer or a healthy child at play. It's quite natural for us to admire and aspire to physical fulfillment. In extreme cases—the rheumatoid arthritis patient who makes it through law school, for instance—we can recognize wonderful courage in someone who is handicapped.[3] But the teaching and tendency in our society is to focus on something other than the body when we talk to people who are physically impaired. Yet so isolated from each other as *people* have we become that if we can't deal with somebody's body, we're often at a loss to deal with them at all.

Stephen Hawking is a good public example. We don't know him personally (I wish!) but we've seen him on television, and watched his disease imprison him more and more securely in a body that can do almost nothing anymore. Yet he remains the world's most brilliant theoretical physicist, and he is still able to share his incredible understanding of the universe with the rest of us through his books. Maybe I *can* hike the quarter mile up the scrabbly slope to the door of the Crystal Cave, but believe me, were I to be privileged to sit next to Dr. Hawking, there is not a chance I would think of myself as more able, not by comparison

---

[3]Debbie A. Weissenberg, who suffered from rheumatoid arthritis, is an example. I met her mother at a Crone's Conference in the Spring of 2002, and Mrs. W. gave me a copy of her late daughter's book, *You'll Never Walk Alone: Hospital Survival Techniques.* For a copy of this short, sweet book with a lively sense of humor, contact Fran Weissenberg at Post Office Box 57070 in Tucson, AZ 85732.

to his pretty much magical understanding of physics, the universe, and everything.

Magic, you will recall, is *the art of changing consciousness at will.* Not the art of changing bone structure or fat distribution or gender or eye color or height or other inherited characteristics at will, not the art of changing environmental hazards or what infuriating thing somebody else decides to do. There are some things we cannot change, and our various disadvantages are among them. What magic can affect is our perception of our difficulties and our options.

For generations, the "norms" of American life were handed down unchanged from parents to children; now many of us lead very different lives than our parents did. We live in different places, with different priorities and different opportunities than our parents had. We make different careers than our parents considered, we create families and relationships very different from the ones our parents showed us. Our children, biological and community, will lead different lives than we do. This is an aspect of rebirth.

Witches celebrate these differences—these rebirths—because Wicca knows that change nourishes growth, and therefore holds change sacred. The society we live in, though, tends to fear changes that challenge established power structures and their institutions. For this reason, it's important that we individually strengthen our most significant and far-reaching decisions—whether they were exactly choices or not—by affirming them (and our authority to make them) ritually. In this way we turn the death that change itself can feel like into the rebirth that change also is.

Whether you're undertaking a new career, making new living arrangements, entering a new relationship or leaving an old one, or making another change in your lifestyle, whether you're giving up an addiction or foreclosing an option after long thought or struggle, you will be more comfortable with your decision or choice or landing if you give it ritual dignity and authority.

The affirmative rituals you devise personally, in the context of your own circumstances, will have the greatest power. I offer this one as an example of the way we can, so to speak, steer into the skid. It can be modified to consecrate any sort of Decision or Choice, any emergence from ordeal or loss, and for use by more than one person.

For this ritual, you will need some modeling clay. Several kinds are available, and any will do. If you are so inclined, you could get "real" clay, the kind you can fire, and later take it to a kiln and have yourself a permanent talisman. You will need at least enough to make a ball two inches in diameter; more is fine.

Preparation

You will need an appropriately colored and anointed candle, matched to the nature of your Choice or Decision, and appropriate incense, both in addition to what you normally use on your altar. You'll also need a greeting card, either one that's blank on the inside or one that says CONGRATULA-TIONS. It should be appropriate to your Decision, and conform to your usual taste in greeting cards. (In other words, if you usually like silly cards, get a silly one; if you usually like hearts and flowers, get hearts and flowers.) Make your own if you like. Remember a pen, pencil, quill, crayon, or something else to write with. Finally, you will need *goodies*! Get something that you really like and don't have very often, something that really tastes like celebration. (Whatever your personal equivalent of champagne and caviar is, get that.)

Set up your altar in the usual way. At the front of the altar, or on a consecrated cloth on a nearby table or on the floor in front of the altar, assemble the modeling clay, Decision candle and incense, greeting card, pen and goodies.

The Ritual

Begin by casting the Circle in your usual way.

Say to the Goddess:

"Mother of Life, as You have given birth to All that Is, so I am giving birth to my life this day. As Your blessing is upon

All You have created in Your love and will, so do I receive Your blessing upon that which I create today from my love and will."

Say to the God:

"Horned One, as You dance, stepping surely to the holy rhythm of life, so I step surely to the rhythm of my own life. You face both joy and sorrow with a brave, adventurous heart, and I share Your courage in the joy and sorrow I feel now."

Say to the Guardians:

"Guardians in the East, my mind is clear and bright and free, swept clean by Your winds, and I rejoice to take the first breath of my new life.

"Guardians in the South, my heart is pure and full of passion, my fear burned away by Your fires, and I rejoice as my heart begins to beat to the rhythm of my Choice.

"Guardians in the West, my soul is calm and full of confidence, my doubt transformed in Your tides, and I rejoice as I embrace my feelings for the first time in my new life.

"Guardians in the North, my foundation is strong and equal to the adventure I have chosen, my body is fortified by Your firm core, and I rejoice as I take control by making this Decision."

Lighting your Decision candle and incense, say to the Gods, the Guardians and all your ancestors and ghosts:

"Now I kindle the hearth-fire of the new life I have [chosen to make]; now I see manifest what I have only felt in the air until now."

Taking up the modeling clay, work it until it is fairly soft, and passing it through the candle-flame and incense, say:

"Now I take my life into my own hands, and consecrate it with my own heart and my own mind, and dedicate it to [say the names you use for the Goddess and the God], the Guardians, and all my ancestors and ghosts."

Now work with the clay, forming a symbol of your Decision. If you are moving, you might make a little house or another symbol of the place you're going. If you're changing jobs, you might make a little desk or some other symbol of the work you'll be doing.

If you're entering a new relationship, you might make a little heart, and so forth. The symbol should be meaningful to you, and never mind whether anybody else can tell what it is or not. You can even make a straightforward talisman if you like and decorate it with a symbol of your Decision.

(If you are using fireable clay, and if you will want to wear your talisman or hang it from a cord or a pouch, remember to make the hole a little bit larger than it needs to be, because it will shrink when it's fired.)

When you have formed your symbol, pass it through the Decision-candle and incense again, and say:

"With this [name what you have made, or call it a talisman or symbol] I affirm and consecrate my decision to [describe your Decision succinctly, clearly and completely] and dedicate this Decision to [the names you use for the Goddess and God, or the aspects you have chosen as appropriate for this ritual]. May this [talisman] be my constant reminder of my Decision and the commitment I have made [to the Gods and] to myself to make this Decision my reality from this day forward, between the Worlds and in all the Worlds."

Now stand up, or stretch up if you are already standing. Holding the talisman up in front of you at arm's length, walk or dance deosil from the East around the Circle, saying,

"My Lady and My Lord, Bléssed Guardians, see! In the East and in the South and in the West and in the North, in Spring and Summer, in Fall and Winter, my Decision [Choice] goes before me and makes a path for me to walk, in every Season, in all the Worlds. As I do will, so mote it be!"

Now set your talisman on the altar. Take a few minutes, if you need to, to contemplate the reality of your decision and the reality of your control over your own life, the nature of your commitment, etc.

When you are ready, write yourself a congratulatory note in the greeting card. Write all the affirmations you need to hear about this Decision and sign your civil name and/or your magical name, whichever is most appropriate to the Decision you have made. Address the envelope to yourself and seal the card inside.

Again, if you need to, take a few minutes to think about your Decision, hug yourself if you want to, hum a little, smile, do a little dance, anything that feels right. When you have finished, offer your celebratory *goodies* to each of the four Directions, and then hold them over the Decision-candle and incense, and say,

"Today I have made a Decision so momentous that my life will never be the same again. In the name of [the Gods] and in the sight of [name the Goddess and God], the Guardians and all my ancestors and ghosts, I have made the decision and commitment to [describe your Decision].

"Thus, in the name of the Gods and before the Gods, the Guardians and all my ancestors and ghosts, I have chosen and consecrated my life. So in this fire and air do I consecrate these cakes and this ale to Gods and to the Decision I have made with Their strengths and blessings."

Leave some of the goodies on the altar for the Gods, or make your libation and offering in your usual way, and enjoy! If it is appropriate, you may wish to share your goodies with your talisman.

When you have finished your celebratory feast, close your Circle in the usual way. When that is done and everything is put away, *put the greeting card in the mail.*

If your talisman is made of fireable clay, let it dry *very* thoroughly before you take it to a ceramics shop to have it fired, because if there is any moisture left in it, it could explode in the kiln, which would not be good.

If you are not going to fire your talisman, then put it on a shelf or, wrapped in a cloth, in a pouch somewhere safe. Whether it is fired or not, get it out and let it recharge you whenever you are feeling small or doubtful, and don't forget to recharge the talisman when you are feeling strong and powerful!

Karma

Affirmations are about attitudes. Our attitudes are all we know we can control (though Lord knows it's hard). Other people's attitudes and other aspects of the mundane world we live in are beyond our control. Wicca is one of the few religions to acknowledge that "stuff" happens, stuff that isn't our karma coming back to bite us, stuff that has its own teeth.

We have told the Explorer since he was very young that there's a difference between things that happen to you and things you do wrong. Making mistakes is not a capital crime. The Goddess asks naught of sacrifice. Even if it was (as Canyondancer grumbled for a while about his back injury) "your own damn fault," our challenges still aren't punishments of any kind, and we will stimulate no growth by imagining that they are.

Further, the nature of life, of Individuality distinguished from Wholeness, is diversity. We know that ancient communities recognized that our worth is not defined by our bodies. There are 60,000 year-old burials of cripples who couldn't have lived without the help of their clans, and who yet lived relatively long lives, and were buried with reverence and the expectation of rebirth.

In those ancient times, when every material need was met by personal physical labor and daring, it must have seemed quite obvious that there was worth in people beyond their physical capacities. Otherwise those unable to contribute materially to the welfare of the tribe might have been left to die. We sometimes still call those ancestors "primitive," yet in this respect, at least, they were far more fully human than we moderns have sometimes been. The Craft both reclaims and recreates this sensibility. Wicca encourages those of us faced with difficult losses to *love* themselves and to *trust* their own worth, and to find the courage to explore and develop other capabilities if the ones we were counting on fail us.

We are taught young to blame somebody or something else when plans or expectations are unfulfilled. This habit enervates us, drains our power through anger and doubt and cynicism. Oddly enough, the more we blame people or circumstances beyond our control, the guiltier we end up feeling. These feelings are normal in a patriarchal, *either/or* society that has developed blaming the victim into an art.

That things don't happen without a reason doesn't mean that there's some master out there in high orbit for whose occult reasons things happen to us. It means that it is our nature to *perceive* meaning. It might be clearer to say that "nothing happens without being given a reason," because putting it that way accommodates the fact that it is we who give our lives meaning. We humans, we're the pattern-seers. It occurs to us to copy geological or meteorological patterns onto pottery or blow ocher at close range to make hand-prints on walls. It occurs to us to think esthetospiritually. We're people who know that the Individuality we are experiencing is Individuality in contrast to a Whole.

Remember the creation story as Starhawk told it, where the Goddess saw Herself and was so taken in the experience as simultaneously Whole and Individual that Her delight manifested in life, the universe and Everything? Well, that isn't any *once upon a time* creation story, not about a literal event fixed in time and space, but about something that happens now, today, this minute, whenever we realize that we are simultaneously Whole and Individual.

Evolution is a fact as far as I'm concerned. The dance, the Polarity, the coming and going, the giant, giant cycles we can't begin to imagine in scope or period, that's not an intellect, not an articulate consciousness. But it evolves (dynamically, not linearly) into one, and we're part of it. Perceiving pattern and meaning is instinctive with us. We all do it differently, but we all do it. When we say *nothing happens but for a reason*, we're really expressing a biological imperative. We put meaning to things so naturally that we don't even know how we do it.

In this context *reason* isn't a *because* cause, it's a *cause* in the *raison d'etre* sense. So looking for *causal* reasons for the bad things that happen to us puts us on the wrong track altogether. When we get back on the right track—when our understanding is consistent with Wiccan principles—we can recognize our grief and confusion as *energy* that we can transform and redistribute. We can transform grief and confusion and anger, but not without acknowledging them. Through the process of grief, we can turn our sadness and anger and fear to something worthwhile in our lives and in the world. We can honor the loved ones we've lost or the dream we've had to give up.

This might mean finishing a project left undone, or starting something new, long-planned or just occurring to you. When you direct your physical and magical energy toward such a memorial goal, that *becomes* the "reason for" your loss. *That's* what "nothing happens but for a reason" means. Let's not forget, either, that single causes are very rare.[1] Most things are more "confluenced" than "caused." Witches find this perspective supported in much of Wiccan liturgy. The Goddess asks naught of sacrifice, remember; and when all things die, the God gives them rest and strength that they may be born again. This cycling process is "all the magic." In other words, this cycling process *is* "the Divine," the God/dess. We are God/dess because we live [in] the cycling process. You might say that the reason things die is that they must die to be reborn; *birth*, not death, is the dominant characteristic of the cycle. To resist death is to deny life.

Grief and fear are powerful, and anger often comes with them. Grieving, fearful, we feel out of control, and nobody likes that

---

[1] Dr. M. Scott Peck, in *A Different Drum* (Touchstone Books, 1987), tells us that the technical psychological term for things having more than one reason for happening is that everything is "overdetermined."

feeling. Anger is a natural response to a feeling of helplessness, and anger can trigger the body chemistry of heroic action. But if there doesn't seem to be anything we can *do*, sometimes that anger gets thrown at the people we think are, or should be, in control. Anger is obviously strong, and blaming somebody else is a hard habit to break, so one of the things children of all ages wonder is whether people can die from angry wishes.

Not directly, the way they can die from bullets, no. Indirectly? Well, remembering the Threefold Law and the Rede, I'd say the caster of a curse is in more danger than any intended victim. As a parent and a priestess, I'd say that *children's* thoughts and feelings are not often under good enough control to be effective as curses. When we're coping with grief-anger, grown-up energy may not be under good enough control to count as a curse, either.

But, when you cast any spell, the energy of your intention is sent forth toward a goal, a "desired result." How much energy you send depends on the intensity of your intent and the degree of change you mean to accomplish. An obsessive long-term intention to cause harm, general or specific, even without being acknowledged in ritual, *is* a curse. Now, you know how much energy it takes to put on a party: you know you're exhausted afterwards, and that's for a *good* "spell." Imagine how much *more* energy it takes to make something really awful happen!

People can conceive and nurture ill intent, of course, but on the whole, the universe being generally bent toward creativity and growth, "evil" is much more difficult to orchestrate than "good," and casting a curse takes a lot of energy. It takes a lot of time, too. The image of the consequence of cursing that sticks in my mind is from an old "Sinbad" movie, in which the evil sorceress's transformations into a seagull used too much of her energy, and she could not bring harm to the hero. She ended up being unable to completely reverse one of her magicks, and she was left with a seagull's foot replacing one of her own. Not only was this pretty inconvenient, it also proved her guilt, and worst of all, from her perspective, Sinbad was *not* defeated.

There is some question, too, whether anyone who thinks that cursing is appropriate has the strength and skill to cast a curse beyond his or her ego-aura. Casting spells of any kind requires an ability to go beyond oneself, and people of a mind to cast curses often have difficulty getting beyond themselves. In my opinion, if you're a healthy Wiccan, you won't be thinking about casting any curses,[2] and you're unlikely to be affected by any either, because your own auras will be strong enough to repel any that get that far.

Kids sometimes wonder whether *their* angers and fears can curse people. You know, the kid's mad at somebody and wishes they'd fall down or something, and then when that person gets hurt or killed in some accident on the freeway, the kid assumes complete responsibility for it. Or the kid doesn't want to go see Gramma in the nursing home, and wishes she would just die, already, and then she does, and the kid thinks s/he killed her.

These are what I call "venting wishes," just little bursts of anger that release some of the enormous energy churning around inside kids whose bodies and feelings are changing just about constantly (no matter how old they are). The anger or fear is real, and it needs to be acknowledged; but the wish for harm only expresses the magnitude of the feeling, not any formal intent to do anyone ill.

Indeed, many times the children who express such wishes do not fully comprehend the workings of cause and effect in human life, and couldn't work the kind of magic they're worried about even if they did want to. Children need to understand that their anger is natural, and that their feelings *cannot* kill other people. Expressing feelings appropriately doesn't harm people either. Children, and that includes our inner children, should be assured that they are not hurting anybody by feeling whatever way they do. We can't *do* whatever we want, but none of our feelings are outlaw.

[2]Some Witches, and I am one of them, think it's alright to curse *practices*. Rape, for instance, child abuse, pollution. What makes this sort of cursing "okay" is that one's intent is actually to *heal*. One of my favorite expressions of this distinction is a button/bumper sticker that says, FIGHT AIDS, NOT PEOPLE WITH AIDS.

Children and Death

In the Wiccan understanding of the world, no life is too short to celebrate. Culturally, we like to think that a kid has her whole life in front of her at least until she's in her early 20's, but if she dies earlier, taking that literally can leave us with a big hole in our lives and not a real clear idea of what used to be there.

When a child dies (or might die, or is dying), our sense of *balance*, personal and cosmic, is affected. The death of a child grotesquely distorts the dance we have come to expect to do with life. In addition to dealing with our personal loss, we are faced with the experience of a sort of an *eddy*, if life's normal progression is like a river. Children are supposed to outlive their parents, not predecease them. When children die, it's easy to get stuck in that hypnotizing eddy, focusing on the swirling spiritual disorientation. It's easy to fight that child's death so hard that you redefine the whole river of life in terms of that one uncharted whirlpool.

It's always painful to "let go" of someone you love. It is even more painful when the person you have to let go of is somebody little, somebody you were supposed to protect and not let anything bad happen to. The guilt that this culture teaches us to feel is particularly heavy when a child dies. "Such a tragedy, *such* a tragedy," people will say when a child dies. "And with his whole life still ahead of him."[1] The common perception is that a child *didn't* lead a whole life if death came to him before he was 25 or so. When someone dies even younger, under five, less than a year, the idea is that the kid never even got the chance to make a mark on life. Until recently, stillborn babies were not always even named, not even acknowledged as having lived at all.

But anyone who has spent any time at all with a baby, really being there *with* a baby—even in utero—or with a young child, knows that we change each other's lives at *every* age. A miscarried fetus, a stillborn baby, an aborted embryo, these people change the world even though they never walk in it. An infant changes us all enormously. And older children have well and truly wrought wonders.

When someone very old dies, we're more inclined to be philosophical. Ah, we muse, s/he's lived a full life, there are many who remember, and s/he will not die alone. Life is good. We could say the same things about most children, if we gave it some thought. Whether we are grieving for children or adults, the process of "letting go" is one of learning to understand as *whole* a life that wasn't "supposed" to be finished yet. There is no comfort in focusing on what could have been or what should have been; and there is no honor to anyone's death in that, either. There were moments, months, years of that life to celebrate!

Letting go is learning to define a loved one's life in its own terms rather than according to conventional expectations, learning to appreciate that life as a meaningful whole. This means unburdening yourself of the prejudices of linear thought. One of the foundations of linear thought is that longer (bigger, costlier, etc.) is better. But if we say that longer lives are "better," then how is a life

---

[1] I say "him" because according to various tables in the *Statistical Abstract of the United States*, published by the U.S. Department of Commerce (Economics and Statistics Administration, Bureau of the Census) in Washington, D.C., this edition in 1991, boys born in 1988 were expected to die at a rate of 9.55 per 1,000 and girls at a rate of 7.47 per 1,000. In 1988, 1,114 out of 100,000 males younger than a year died, while only 898 out of 100,000 females under the age of one year died.

worth anything if it is short? Children (and the elderly and the handicapped) often suffer the same disrespectful indignities in life as they do in death: they are too small or quiet to be seen and heard . . . or housed or clothed or fed or healed. And when they die, we usually mourn their deaths, but we *don't* usually celebrate their lives because we keep thinking "their whole lives were ahead of them" or that they "never had a real chance to live."

Among my acquaintances is a nurse-midwife who has attended stillbirths and sorrowful terminations of pregnancies. She knows how important it is to acknowledge any baby's reality and worth. Babies that are born dead, or born pre-viable and allowed to die, are our children, too. In the hospital where my friend works, these babies are footprinted, gowned, and photographed. When the grieving mother goes home with her baby's blanket and other souvenirs, the grief she feels is authenticated, so she can deal with it and redirect and ground her energy through the process of grief. My friend's experience is that a mother's sharing her grief with her other children, with the rest of her family, helps all of them to work through the pain.

Pain worked through can be transformed into strength. The family that grieves together is strengthened and tempered; and if they are guided by Wiccan thealogy and philosophy, their appreciation of life can deepen.

Canyondancer and I accepted the Explorer as a whole, real, feelings-counting and opinions-mattering guy from the beginning, and that's still working out pretty well. If he died, we'd be devastated, but we would also have a sense of his life as complete—because we *already* have a sense of his life as a whole, having a meaningful effect in the world. We have seen him grow taller than we are from the milli-small zygote he was at his conception. We've watched him develop interests into skills. We've seen him learn to set goals and achieve them. He's taught us a good deal about ourselves, too.

He's grown now, so his accomplishments are easy to see, but even fetuses change us—"She changes everything She touches, and everything She touches changes," Starhawk's popular chant reminds us. Those changes, like cool but invisible breezes, merit our attention and respect as much as any changes we can send pictures of to the grandparents.

The only way to improve the experience of a child's death is to improve our relationship with children, and that means valuing them because they are celebrations incarnate, literally. But until we choose to be—as a society, as a planet—inspired by children's innocent energy and expectations, nothing will change; and *not changing* is a fate a lot worse than death.

In helping children interpret deaths they experience—their own and/or the deaths of playmates, pets, siblings, other relatives, or neighbors—the best we can do is share our own interpretations. We can respect their worry that the same thing could happen to them and reassure them according to the circumstances. We can talk with them as much as they want us to about what we think it all *means*. People sometimes shy from this, believing that children "cannot understand" or "should not be made to deal with it." Very often, these grown-ups' real reluctance is to face their own mortality. They can't share their feelings about death because they don't know for sure what their feelings are.

It's nigh unto impossible to keep your feelings from your kids. *Something* will get through to them, and they're likely to think it's about them if you don't tell them any different. (This is true of friends your own age, too, and your parents, and everybody who cares.) So if you try to keep your grief from your children, you're likely to leave them scared and alone, feeling like you're mad at them for something they can't imagine. If that feeling becomes associated with the death, they may feel somehow responsible. This is not a very nice way to feel no matter how old you are.

It is far better to share your uncertainty than to hide it from your children. If you admit that you're sad or scared or angry, your kids will know that their feelings are okay, too. They'll learn, too, that strong feelings don't have to keep people apart. Understanding exactly what you're facing is less important than knowing there's somebody you can trust facing it with you.

When our old Siamese cat died a few years ago, the kids in the neighborhood came by to pay their respects, bringing rocks from the desert to line the grave we were digging in the yard. We talked to them a little about death, about the Summerland, and mainly about the pouch of grave-goods they were watching me get ready. And as I spoke to them, I cried.

Instead of covering my face and withdrawing from conversation, though, as many of us were brought up to do, I kept right on going, clearing my throat and wiping my nose when I needed to. They asked me if I would miss my old cat, and I said I thought I would, but that I was comforted to know that we'd given her our true attention these many years. Because none of us had taken her for granted, none of us felt any *guilt* about her death.

The way we acted—involving those kids in our funeral preparations, talking to them through tears, and sharing our feelings—showed these kids that death *is* sad, definitely sad, but not scary, *and* that being sad doesn't invalidate a person. The things I said to them made sense, even though there were tears streaming down my face as I spoke (and even though my Wiccan belief that animals have souls may well contradict what their religions teach). My sorrow did not diminish my authority, and I am glad that these children have that experience to counter the social conventions of death.

The Explorer's friends' contributions to the funeral process gave them some sense of participation, and a way to ground the energy that the sight of death raises in us all. Unless we have something to do, some outlet for the energy, we may find it distressing, unnerving, restless-making. In the old days, we baked pies and casseroles for bereaved neighbors. We took care of their kids, we pitched in on their harvest, we fed the stock, and did whatever work they couldn't finish. And in the old days, too, the bereaved had more to do physically. People of all ages *still* need to be actively involved in the deaths that touch their lives. This is not a search for total mastery over death, just for some sense of belonging to it.

Belonging, yes. The mainstream culture tells us that we want to put as much distance as we can between death's camp and our tents. But all the scary stories and horrifying lies have never been able to completely dispel older, gentler images of death: the gentle hands of Thanatos still part soft curtains for some of us. The truth is that death *is* just a door, and there *aren't* any terrifying specters behind it really, just the close-holding, swaddling Womb of the Universe, the Void from which we are continually created, Wholeness—that for which we long, that to which we belong.

Longing is what leads us ever between the Poles, and the Pole toward which we lean from Individuality and its mortal perspective is Wholeness. Death is the Door to Wholeness, the Door that opens upon Youth. So although it saddens us—a response initiated by the limbic system, instinctive chemistry that contributes to the continuation of the species—even when that Door opens to *a* youth, we yet may find cause to celebrate. Mortality is a necessary condition of Individuality; and as above, so below: death is as magnificent for the individual who is dying as it is resonant in the Whole which receives her. Death is as much in the service of Individual life as it is in the service of life as a Whole.

Canyondancer and I have never promised the Explorer that we'll never die, or that we'll never let anything bad happen to him. We've said that we'd try, and even admitted that we'd die for him; but we never promised that bad stuff wouldn't happen. We did, however, promise to face the bad stuff together. The Explorer insisted, when he was very young, on a funeral for his Jack o' Lantern. We buried Jack with His candle still burning, and it was really very touching.

If children were allowed to discover and explore their mortality—burying family pets in the yard, going to Aunt Fay's funeral—then they could learn to work with that reality, rather than squirming in fear of it. There's no need for fear of death (although the ways we can die nowadays are pretty scary), and so it needn't be "icky" to give children simple training in basic deathing. Children appreciate being empowered just as much as grown-ups do, maybe more. Being able to settle your own fears by remembering you know how to deal with the scary stuff is a prerequisite to adulthood in the species and full spirituality beyond that.

So you can write a meditation that takes you flying out of your body, and through some kind of gathering, narrowing tunnel with tantalizing distractions from the almost painfully bright light in the center. Soar determinedly directly toward the center of the brightest light—and see what you find beyond. Include the other half of this exhilarating journey: from the worlds behind the center of the brightest light, you can soar back, through a darkening tunnel, back to the brightness of the center of the living room. Death and rebirth. You can't have one without the other.

Children, who still have a wide peninsula between their right and left brains, appreciate the balance you achieve when you present death and rebirth as a pair, as complements. Facing death, we are living mythically, we are between the Worlds, and children sometimes have the steadier feet in these realms. But we cannot accept their blessing—cannot even recognize it—if we are consumed with guilt for being grown-up yet unable to save a child.

Living mythically, which facing death demands of you, the rules are changed a little. One of the changes is that you accept everybody as an equal. You value their knowledge without prejudice against anyone, because you never know who will be the Gods in disguise. So you don't blow off what children have to say, at least not without consideration; and when mythic duty thus calls you to hear what children have to say, you may find out that they've pretty well got it handled. We can learn from children's observations of death, even if society acts like older means wiser automatically. Children in the Nazi death camps scratched outlines of butterflies on the barracks' wooden walls.[2] I believe they understood death as metamorphosis, as becoming. And rightly so.

We can tell our children the truth about death only if we can move beyond our own fears of it. Otherwise, we shackle them with the very same collars of fear that we bemoan wearing. And that goes for our "inner children" as well as for our kids.

Another unpleasant-to-think-about death that involves children is abortion. To the best of our collective knowledge, "witches" have practiced abortion for thousands of years, so it must have been the consensus of our ancestors that ending a pregnancy was not sacrilegious. I cannot believe that we could have been as herbally sophisticated as our ancestors were without developing a corresponding spiritual sophistication with regard to the ancient idea that life feeds on life.

There is no footing in Wiccan thealogy or history for a stand against abortion; neither does Wicca encourage abortion. We hold life sacred, and the Goddess asks naught of sacrifice. One of Wicca's premises is that the female principle is generative, and one of the ways we express this is in a respect for women's autonomy.

One factor seldom addressed is *access to resources*. (This is an interesting dimension of *any* social problem, actually.) It takes a lot to raise a child. Yes, it takes money, and that is a problem for some parents. But it takes more than money and more than the food, shelter, and clothing money can buy. It takes some living skills and some discipline and some patience. These skills, that discipline and the patience are neither taught in schools nor valued by our culture. This institutionally-directed diminution of personal responsibility is unforgivable.

My personal opinion is that when women have access to the resources we need to raise healthy babies, when we can get equal pay for equal work—when there *is* work, and safe day care, and

---

[2]In *On Death and Dying* and other work, Elisabeth Kübler-Ross writes about this; now and again you see it in shows on PBS and other places.

when we live in decent places and eat well and don't have to worry about rape and our children being kidnapped—*then* you will not hear so much about abortion.

It is, however, a choice women have virtually always been able to make, and a choice rightly ours to make.[3] *How* we should choose in any given instance is much harder to say. Indeed, it's a Guardian-facing sort of choice, and each of us who makes it must, ultimately, make it on our own authority and responsibility.

Harm none? Doesn't abortion harm the fetus? I've always looked at abortion as one of the ways a mom sometimes has to say "no" to our children. Our souls come back again and again, and abortion doesn't co-opt all a soul's choices. There is nothing in Wiccan thealogy that specifically forbids abortion, nor anything that especially encourages it. There is support, however, for understanding each woman as having the right and obligation to make her choice according to her conscience.

---

[3]Acknowledging a woman's birth-right to choose isn't a decision "for" or "against" abortion. There's the question of whether a woman has the right to abort a pregnancy or not, and then there's the separate question of how she should exercise that right. It's like the difference between whether women have the right to vote, and who you think we should vote for once it's established that we do. I think the right to choose is too natural to fall into legal jurisdictions. Abortion is between me and the Goddess, not between me and society.

Suicide

Suicide's another decision left to conscience. There are so many circumstances, so many experiences, so many souls to search . . . is it possible to know whether and when suicide is right or wrong? How do you tell? Witchcraft has no universal Book or global High Priestess to proclaim our truths. No, our individual discoveries of the truth are at the core of Wicca. So how do you tell?

Most of us know that we're supposed to take *any* suicide threat seriously, and most of us do; most of us are also unqualified to offer heavy-duty psychological/psychiatric counseling. The cultural attitude that life and death are subordinate to our immediate personal gratification is certainly *not* in the service of life. Does this make somebody who threatens to or actually does kill himself an infidel or a bad person? Well, no.

The person who approaches suicide manipulatively or as a solution to the thousand natural shocks the flesh is heir to[1] is feeling unconnected, has become disoriented. Whether this is a singular "glitch" or part of a pattern may be hard to determine, but a threat or attempt at suicide from this perspective certainly merits attention.

Initiating a crisis intervention by paramedics (police officers often accompanying them) is pretty sure to draw an angry response, too. This anger is an aspect of denial, although knowing this makes it very little easier to bear. Confronting it, you'll prob-

[1] William Shakespeare, *"Hamlet,"* act III, scene One. My copy is *The Complete Works of William Shakespeare*, edited by W. G. Clark and W. Aldis Wright (Nelson Doubleday, in New York). A famous consideration.

ably have intense feelings of your own. One of those feelings may be helplessness, for it's true that you can't always save your friends.

Yet if our friends do things that alarm us and our companions, we *do* have a right to bring it up. I call it an *obligation* of friendship, and of companionship in the Craft, to share concerns; and to *act*, if what you see looks like an emergency. Wondering in agony why you didn't call 911 is a much bigger risk than anyone's anger about an unnecessary call. Loss of friendship is less than loss of friends' lives.

We don't have to depend entirely on our own sense of whether someone's suicide is a "threat" or a legitimate plan: our liturgies give us some clues. Age and fate, the Descent[2] reveals, are the causes of death. "As I will, so mote it be," we proclaim. That we can be the authors of our own fate is a fundamental assumption of Wicca, both materially and morally. I take this to mean that a decision to commit suicide is not necessarily an affront to the Goddess.

We all know there are certain circumstances that make suicide comprehensible. Incurable, incapacitating, degenerative diseases, comas that entangle a soul in tubes and wires, pain so debilitating that humanity surrenders. Whether we like the idea or not, we find it almost easy to understand suicide in such cases. Sometimes there's not a big difference between "suicide" and "No, let's not attach those things in the first place." More and more people are writing living wills so that they *won't* be subjected to any misplaced heroism. People tend to think of living wills in terms of sudden, gory automobile accidents, but they apply equally to circumstances of progressive illness or disease.

The example the Gods give us of "right dying" is the God's death in the service of life. It seems to me that when a person can realistically anticipate being incapacitated by progressive, incurable diseases or faces other debilitating and irremediable degener-

---

[2] *The Descent of the Goddess* is the story of the Goddess' descent into the Underworld to ask the Lord why He made all things that She loved die. A version of it is given at the beginning of Part One.

ation, suicide might be a viable option. I know that I would consider it if I could no longer contribute to my communities.

Don't get me wrong. I expect to live to a hundred years or
more, and I expect to need progressively more help as I get older
and older. When that happened to one of my grandmothers, she
felt weakened by it, ashamed to be dependent. But I am *proud* to
be interconnected, and the kind of "no longer able to contribute" I'm talking about here is the needing-around-the-clock-care
and being unable to write or converse or communicate or share
awareness with the rest of the world anymore kind.

Sometimes bodies get stuck being kept alive, and I believe that's
at least extremely frustrating to the soul forcibly detained by tubes
and wires. About the only way we have now to indicate with any
authority that we do not wish to be kept alive by extraordinary
means is to sign a living will. (You can get one of these from just
about any Memorial Society, and Memorial Societies will be listed
in your business white pages or in your Yellow Pages. The Hemlock
Society in Los Angeles also provides useful information; so does
the Society for the Right to Die, headquartered in New York.)

I think most Wiccans would agree that there are circumstances
under which suicide is a reasonable option. There are also circumstances in which choosing to die is *not* in the service of life.
In order to distinguish between those circumstances we need to be
a little more clear in our understanding of "in the service of life."

Well, "service," according to my ancient dictionary,[3] is "work
done or duty performed for another or others," and rarely or
archaically, "respect, attention, devotion, as of a lover to his lady."
(I am not making this up!) I tend to combine these definitions
myself, thinking of "service" as work and duty in devotion to the
Lady—who is, after all, Life Herself. So "death in the service of
life" is about accepting death as a part of life, so that dying well
and gracefully is a devotion to the Lady. This romantic approach is

---

[3] *Webster's New World Dictionary of the American Language* (World Publishing Co., Cleveland
and New York, 1962).

comforting, and there's nothing wrong with it, as long as we don't stay on its surface forever.

What exactly does "dying well and gracefully" mean?

To me, it means dying unencumbered with fears and annoyances, dying in peace and unafraid, dying with confidence that this life was honorable and productive, dying in perfect trust of rebirth through the Mother. It also means being able, or trying, anyway, to orient yourself toward your own death and participate actively in it, mindful of the effect your present death will have on your next incarnation. And, 'dancer and I think it requires some consideration of the effect it will have on our present companions, who were before and will be our companions again.

I think that when a suicide releases a soul imprisoned by an incurably incapacitated body, or from a body that soon will be incapacitated, or from any medically irretrievable situation, it's in the service of life. The intention of the act is to return the Individual's energy to the universe, restore it to Wholeness, whence it can Individualize again in another life. In some cases, when natural progress around the Wheel has been interrupted, suicide can restore the balance.

This sort of suicide, brave and noble, should not only not be abhorred or prohibited, it should be ritualized and shared. It's difficult and hazardous to arrange a public suicide: legal consequences are inconsistent among the states, the medical establishment is nervous and divided, and it's just plain distasteful to some people. However, there is no reason not to celebrate a sort of requiem *with* an individual who has chosen suicide.[4] Adventure's attitude is that any time you part from someone could be the last time; and certain farewells face greater-than-ordinary risks. Adventurers feast together before riding off alone into the dawn toward the mysterious castle and its unknown guardian who beckons from that distant hill.

[4] The Paramount film *Harold and Maude*, released to home video in 1979, has an interesting perspective on this idea, though Maude's choice has always seemed a little too arbitrary and inflexible for my taste.

As I write (in 1998), Oregon's assisted suicide law is under attack by the federal government. The argument is that it opens the door to euthanasia, and will allow families to condemn to "suicide" members who are old and in the way, or whose illnesses will be expensive. But the provisions of the law belie that. Two or more doctors must affirm that the illness is terminal, and the patient must ask at least twice, once at least 10 days later than the first time.

In my own experience, the danger with this law is that too many people will still be forced to suffer through long and painful deaths. My mother was diagnosed, after months of tests, with pancreatic cancer. It's untreatable, and painful. She wanted to choose the moment of her death, and to go before she was at the bitter end. Unfortunately, her doctor admitted her to a Catholic hospital. By the time she was moved to a nursing home, she didn't have the 10 days of lucidity she needed between her two requests to die.

If there'd been time, her doctors would have prepared an IV, and she herself would have chosen the moment to let the morphine come to her and take her gently into death. As it was, her pain became unbearable, she drifted in and out of lucidity, in and out of anger and fear. Instead of sending her off gently with one dose, we had to pump her full of a morphine derivative one small unit at a time, a little more every 15 minutes. It took 34 hours to release her spirit from her body, and they were agonizing hours for her.

Do I wish she'd been able to go sooner, the way she wanted to? Of course. It was awful to see her suffer—to *feel* her suffer as her hand clutched at mine. Do I cherish the extra time the legal snafu gave me with her? You bet I do. I had the chance to promise her that she wasn't going to be "in trouble" when she died. Frankly, it was hard to tell which pleased her most, that promise or my assurance—to her worry about not having dyed her hair lately— that her natural hair color *wasn't* ugly. I found her smiles in response to both conversations beautiful, almost beatific. I still feel both honored and blessed to have had those last 34 hours with her, but damn, I'd have been honored and blessed to witness her die comfortably and according to her own wishes, too.

If we Circle together before one of us (Wiccans) undertakes death's adventure, the guest of honor can bestow her blessings upon the community and receive the community's affection in return. S/he can bequeath her tools and Book of Shadows if s/he is so inclined, too, and feel free to share her wisdom as well. The community could, at a later hour, perhaps a designated hour, gather again to send more farewell energy from a Circle smaller by one, and yet enlarged.

But if a suicide occurs for reasons that you and others find unacceptable, in circumstances that preclude any celebration, then you must consider that it may *not* be in the service of life. A suicide in the service of life is respectful and expresses devotion. It involves the community in growth as well as sorrow. It sets an example of courage and responsibility for others to follow. A death that is *not* in the service of life leaves you ungrounded and without peace.

In the case of unexpected death, it is often left to survivors to determine how that death serves life, how its energy can be transformed. Recycling the energy released by death, when we do it consciously, as an act of will, is powerful sympathetic magic that facilities a person's dying. In the case of planned suicide, that responsibility falls on the one who has chosen to die. Wicca puts no absolute sanction on suicide, but the standard of Wicca's Rede seems to impose some restrictions. If you want to do a thing as radical as kill yourself, you must consider how this will affect your community, and you must at least suggest a workable alternative attitude to your friends' predictable opposition.

Wiccan belief in reincarnation makes it reasonable to take your own life, or *give* it, depending on circumstances and perspective, if doing so will facilitate your rebirth and your growth through future lives. But our commitment to personal responsibility makes it unreasonable for a Wiccan to commit suicide with the expectation of "leaving it all behind." There's no oblivion, and you can't just abandon the problems attendant on life. You have to resolve them, if not in this life, then in the next, or the next.

We're here because we committed ourselves to another experience of Individuality. Now, nobody chooses abuse and misery. What we really choose is the opportunity to live and learn. I think it's worthwhile, therefore, to look for the hidden—occult!—opportunity in each incarnation, trusting that if you recognized it once, you can know it again, and remember.

There is a range of problems that people everywhere share, and it's petty, I think, to mind which are harder or easier to bear. Many of our dissatisfactions, whatever they are, can be dealt with in one way or another. Sometimes the situation requires correcting information, sometimes it requires "elbow grease," sometimes it requires a discipline of will or facing a Guardian; and sometimes it requires changing time frames or other expectations. But most of our problems *can* be resolved successfully.

Death is life, and if we don't die we can't be reborn, so suicide might be alright when the time for death has come but the doors are or soon will be barred by tubes and wires. In some cases, like my mother's, I think suicide is a responsible decision. When suicide is a short-cut, though, when it just seems easier, or when it is only the logical extension of cynicism, or extreme passive-aggressive manipulation, then my priestess-counsel is that it is a serious mistake, with serious consequences.

One of the fundamental premises of magic is that how we experience the world influences our description of it, and conversely, how we describe the world influences our experience of it. This is why talking about problems and learning to see daunting tasks as a series of smaller jobs are helpful strategies; this is why group therapy works so often.

Covens, of course, are groups, and we already know that we can heal each other to some degree. It is important to understand that *covens are not therapy groups.* Covens cannot be expected to treat psychiatric injuries, any more than High Priestesses who are not doctors aren't expected to set broken bones. Covens can, however, be holistically sensitive, and it is also true that many Wiccan rituals are supportive of recovery.

There are no Psychiatric Tradition covens that I know of. Covens form to work people's magic, not professional magic, and to celebrate the cycles of life and death we revere as holy. It is often remarked that Wiccans do not proselytize, that we draw converts by setting examples of serenity and success. This is one of the ways that Witches heal. When we live as anchors, grounded, persistent in our demonstration that this system of beliefs and practices *does* generate a "kinder, gentler" life and death and rebirth, our lives are living health spells.

We cannot live other people's lives for them, though. We can't face anybody's Guardians for them. Initiation is not by proxy. All we can offer is help, many kinds of help; we cannot offer salvation. Why is that? It is, I would say, because there is no salvation to offer. And why is *that*? *That* is because there is nothing to be saved *from*. There is only experience to have and from which to learn. Suicide can be a legitimate experience, I think, and there is certainly much to be learned from it, for everyone concerned.

There come several times in every life when we must set off on our own explorations of the world, stop working from other people's definitions of the world and begin to think for ourselves and to act from our own intuitions. We re-enter that exploratory, learn-from-our-mistakes stage time and time again throughout our lives.

Every exploration includes risk. The first time that some "tenderfoots" came with Campsight to celebrate Ostara in Crystal Cave,[5] I was with one of them in a narrow side-chamber. She was backing down a shaft that turned out not to connect with the chamber we wanted to reach, when suddenly she mistook her footing. From my position, her safety was obvious, though I moved behind her in case she stumbled backward onto a particularly sharp outcropping. From

[5] Crystal Cave is in the Chiricahua Mountains southeast of Tucson, and is one of only four quartz crystal caves in the continental U.S. It is a fairly large cave, and though the opportunities to get actually lost are limited, it would be possible. There is a very real potential for serious injury, too, and exploring this cave is genuinely risky. Not without taking some of those risks do you reach the rooms where fear becomes reverence. In this cave, it's easy to "flash" onto the ancestral awe that Les Trois Frères and other European caves inspired.

her perspective, she was *definitely* going to fall and die, and it was clear from her expression that she was living, for the moment, from that premise. (Having had my own such experience a few years before, I knew what she was going through.)

In just a split second, her boots were back on solid bedrock, her shoulder only painfully wrenched, not separated or otherwise seriously hurt, and after a couple of relieved exhalations and my showing her where she'd really been, we rejoined the rest of our party, she with a fine story to tell.

Well, life is like that. The things that happen to us that we call lousy—the setbacks, the losses, the humiliations, the betrayals and disappointments, the mistakes, the misunderstandings, the disagreements—those are like the outcroppings and crevasses in Crystal Cave. And like the dangerous and challenging places in the cave, it's often as not life's narrow, scary tunnels that lead us to the most beautiful sparkling places.

The theory is that we accepted the risks along with the rewards when we were born into these lives, that risks and rewards comprise the Individual experience. There's no wide agreement on just how, by what means or process we choose to be reborn, but it's ridiculous at best, and cruel at worst, to think we come back just for the hassles. Generally, the idea is that we come back to a life that will pose us some interesting challenges, to lives that will give us a chance to learn and grow. You have to trust yourself, trust that there *are* opportunities in your life, and find them. But in this mistrustful society that defines "opportunity" so narrowly, that can be hard. Sometimes it can seem impossible.

Wicca does not recognize sin or evil as natural forces,[6] and I do

---

[6]Researchers first thought wild chimps made idyllic societies, later to find that chimpanzee troupes experience disorders too. Yes, and some lambs are born with two heads, and there are connected twins, too. All of this is a function on this plane of the nature of life in three dimensions. Energy becomes material according to certain rules and under certain conditions, some of which we understand and some of which we don't. Remember Gregor Mendel, the botanist, and the sweet peas? If we expect a certain distribution of aberration genetically, physically, why should we be surprised to find it in other dimensions of our lives as well? It's just part of the variation that makes being here interesting, not the signature of any supernatural malignancy.

not know any Wiccans who talk about our mistakes in those terms. But the choice to avoid a responsibility in this life is *also* a choice to face that responsibility in another; and the more lives in which you avoid a given sort of experience, the more obsessed and burdened your future lives become with that choice.

What the God shows us every year is that you can't get away from your mortal responsibility. You can run, but you can't hide, as the saying goes. You can do it well or poorly, "the easy way or the hard way," as we used to say to the Explorer. Your body will die and you will be reborn because that is the nature of everything that takes form in the Universe. Suicide is a viable option when it's the equivalent of a Cesarian section, done to assist the rebirth of a spirit into Wholeness. Suicide is *not* okay when it's done just to sneak out on circumstances you'd rather not face.

We all live under many circumstances over which we have no practical control. What we *can* (learn to) control is our response to these circumstances. Our childhood is longer than the other mammals' because this and the other things we have to learn take some time—and experience—to master. And this capacity, facilitated and affirmed by our cerebral cortex, is one of the most precious gifts (tools) the Gods have given us. Its competent use is natural to humanity,[7] and someone who no longer has competent use of his self-control—of his will, if you want to use the magical term—needs help.

Teenagers tend to think that everything they think and feel is It, because puberty intensifies their senses. They are living in the heart of each moment, and their perspective is an extreme close-up. They are easily overwhelmed, for all their displays. A lot of them take their own lives every year. As we grow older, our hormones usually settle down and we can take a longer view of our

---

[7] Talking about this sort of thing always sets me to hummin' Isaac Bonewits's "The Wizard," a parody of Kenny Rogers's "The Gambler." The relevant line of Isaac's is this: "the Gods gave you your magics well knowin' you was mortal, expecting little save that you would try to use them right." I have this wonderful song on "Be Pagan Once Again," which I think is a great little album.

lives. This doesn't mean we lose the capacity to live intensely in the moment, though, and anytime that we do that wholeheartedly, we can find ourselves overcome. When we do it in Circle, drawing down, or in meditation, or by chanting or dancing, we do not so much *lose* control as make an offering of it to God/dess, trusting that it will be rightly used and restored to us; this is another echo of death and rebirth. If we are inexperienced or undisciplined or lax, though, or forget what's sacred or lose the perspective of Wholeness, being overwhelmed is frightening.

Yet the potential we have to work magic with our pooled energy is immeasurable. In our Wiccan community here, we celebrate our different Traditions, our different calls and chants and correspondences. When we meet in inter-Trad Circles, we thrive on our differences: everybody's raising their own full power in their own way, and when we bring that power together, we make very powerful Sabbats.

But what do we do in the secular world with this precious potential for power? We *damp* it, that's what we do. We suppress it. We kill it. We deaden our children (I mean the whole country "we," not individual parents), smothering them with designer shoes and pants and tops and hats and hair and jargon. We lead them to believe that they are individually powerless, and that their uniqueness diminishes them.

Dancing with Death

Why do "we" do this? For the same reason that the Church burned "us," I'm afraid. We do it because any large group of people whose self-esteem is high and who are proud to be distinctive individuals, who are free to recognize their callings and brave enough to face their Guardians . . . any group of people like that is a threat to the status quo. (It doesn't have to be a big group, either. It wasn't anywhere near a majority of Boomers whose protest work ended the Vietnam war and deposed Nixon.)

Maybe it's the millennium, which has an effect beyond its particular year. History records that strange things happen in times like this, when time is turning. Interest in the planet's ecosystem is growing, concern for a more equitable distribution of food and other resources is growing, investigation of renewable energy sources is proceeding. People are thinking about the transition to the future. Interestingly, people seem to be in general agreement that the future will be unpolluted of air and water, economically just, and politically inclusive and united. Most of us share a vision of the future in which Wiccans will be accorded as much respect as followers of any other faith. And most of us share an awareness that what we do, each of us, now, today, is a step on our way there.

Being a Witch doesn't mean you can heal everybody of everything with a wave of the ol' magic wand. Unfortunately, knowing that—even accepting that—can't always protect you from that nasty feeling of helplessness when friends are in trouble and there seems to be nothing you can do. But of course there *is* always something. (It's really more a question of what we count as "doing," and Witches tend to count more.)

Working with energy, shaping it and directing it, is the business of every Witch. The energy any death raises is intense, so intense that it can take more than one person to handle it. No Wiccan need ever feel shame or guilt about asking for help. We are not limited to Pagan resources, either. We are free to seek counseling from non-Wiccan professionals, for instance, if we want to understand the psychology better; if we are to know what all the tubes and wires are for; if we want to explore healthy ways to express our own feelings.

Nor need any Wiccan priest/ess or group feel resourceless. If you don't know what to say when you gather to send supportive energy or to mourn, don't say anything. Chant. The "Triple Goddess" chant, a combination of "Goddess is alive, magic is afoot" with "We all come from the Goddess" and the "Isis, Astarte," carried on for several minutes (10 at least, and beyond that, as long as you can sustain it) is very grounding and reconnecting. Chanting it while you move, on a route of some kind or in a circle, is comforting and empowering.

I can recommend John Bradshaw's *Homecoming*, especially to leaders of covens. This is a book about rebirth, about "reclaiming and championing your inner child," the subtitle says. Everybody was raised wrong at least a little bit, and this book is full of really terrific exercises, solitary and group, to correct those errors.[1]

---

[1]It's been suggested that all these books about how badly we were all raised are so much bunk, that we ought to stop thinking of ourselves as wounded and get back to being good old-fashioned spunky. One thing the critics seem to be forgetting is that since the 1950s when the interstate highway system was completed and modern American life began to disperse across the country—tearing apart extended families and marooning people in suburbs with all the modern conveniences—not many of us have much more than our families' feedback on which to build our self-esteem. Most of us don't clear the land or plant the crops or tend the beasts much anymore, so there's no sense of accomplishment or evidence of competence about which we can feel good even if our parents don't tell us we are. The violence we complain about on the streets happens in our hearts, too, and a lot of us are just as wounded on the inside as gunshot victims are on the outside. It is true that we need to recover from these wounds and that spunk can be healing, and it's true that our wounds have been inflicted by the system as well as by the people who trashed us or tossed us around. In days to come we may find new ways of healing these wounds, but to deny that we've been hurt is insensitive and out of touch.

(A good many of the group exercises couldn't be *much* more appropriate if they had been written by experienced priest/esses specifically for coven use, even though Bradshaw was a Catholic seminarian.) Confidently, non-blamingly, these exercises re-empower everybody who participates, and raise intense emotional energy to be reconfigured and redirected.

We can work our magics with these exercises, and the ones we write ourselves, to strengthen individuals' self-images and reinforce our groups' foundations. When events are beyond our control, faith-reaffirming rituals are in order to help us deal with the physio-/cultural sense of helplessness. Rebirthing rituals, not formal Initiations but acknowledgment that we all sometimes feel as though we'd like—or have been thrust into—a whole new life, may also be useful. There is much that a creative community can do to steady itself, many yet-to-be-written rituals that will invigorate us. Like most rituals do, these will need to come from our experience, and it will take time.

Anyone dealing with the issues surrounding death today is a pioneer, a forward scout. Not everyone dealing with these issues today *wants* a pioneer's responsibility—to leave some signs beside the trail for those who'll be following, to leave some record of experience on which others can build. Not all of us want to share our feelings about death; not everyone will write a ritual; not each of us who writes a ritual will publish it. Not many of our rites are published yet, but more and more appear in print in local, regional, and national newsletters. Wicca's earlier generations rebirthed our religion, and our contributions nurture it, preparing it for the future. No matter how or when we die, we are all the future.

Even without leaving stone arrows or diaries or our Books, though, we all change the environment for those who follow us. Our "vibes," if you will, linger, marking the psychic terrain like cats and dogs mark the neighborhood. As the Wiccan clergy addresses death more publicly and more thoroughly, as understandings and customs develop, Witches will find more resources available to them.

The Mundane Arrangements

There are not many romantic metaphors for the nitty-gritty practicalities of death, the coffins and insurance policies and subscriptions to be canceled. They intrude like a Monday morning on half-numbed states of grief, and they are insistent. It is in making "the arrangements" that we are most vulnerable—and most noble. Knowing what to expect, in vocabulary and strategy, can be helpful.

Most states, if not all, have what is called in Arizona the "State Board of Embalmers and Funeral Directors." Through that agency, whatever it's called where you live, you can and should get a pamphlet that summarizes your state's funeral regulations. This summary will clarify the circumstances under which bodies must be embalmed, how remains or cremains may be disposed of, and other technicalities around which funeral arrangements must be made.

It is a good idea to understand these legal requirements before you are bereaved or working with grieving family members, because after a death there are some time constraints, and you will not be in the most objective frame of mind. If you are already familiar with the laws, you and those you counsel are less likely to be bamboozled.

What are the funeral decisions that need to be made when someone dies? Immediately, you'll probably have to call an ambulance to take the body from the place of death to a medical facility, if death didn't occur in a hospital. Generally, an autopsy will be done; that's *not* reserved for cases of foul play.

If you are the next of kin, or advising the next of kin, you may be asked about organ donation. This is something that you should consider carefully, and something about which you should share your personal feelings and decision with other people. If you are other people's priest/ess, you may be asked to witness their preferences, too. (In "Some Things to Think About," p. 182, you'll find a partial list of the sorts of things you'll need to think about if you're working with a death.)

People need a wide latitude for the expression of grief. In this authoritarian culture, people are too often intimidated and the funeral arrangements turn out to be less than satisfactory. For Wiccans this is a particular risk, because our rites and symbols are still unfamiliar to the general public. We may make ourselves particularly vulnerable to intimidation if we wait until we are bereaved to begin considering what arrangements to make; and the modifications we might want to make to conventional arrangements take some time to fulfill, so it makes some sense to get some of the work out of the way before anybody dies.

Researching this book, I read a wonderful one by Deborah Duda: *A Guide to Dying at Home.* I recommend this book, obscure though it may be, to anyone even wondering about home death, and certainly to anyone planning one. Home deaths are even stranger to the public understanding than home births. People think death is icky, the same way they think birth is icky; but there is, on the whole, less blood and green slime in both than people expect. Considering dying at home requires re/consideration of the funeral and burial customs most of us take for granted, and widens our horizon to include things like waking and burying family in the back forty.

An advantage of a *Wiccan's* dying at home is the freedom to do as much ritual as s/he likes, whenever s/he likes. The other advantages of home death include the freedom from institutional schedules and regulations, better food, and the surround of love. The advantages to the family of S/he Who Dies At Home are freedom from guilt, the opportunity to offer *other* people the opportunity to share the passage, and the generally lower expense of caring for people at home—if enough people can participate.[1] Coming home to die means that the death is accepted, and that you're no longer trying to save the body, but only to keep the person as comfortable and participating in life as much as s/he can and wants to. Sometimes it's beyond a family's emotional or material resources; sometimes the patient is more comfortable in a hospital or nursing home. Dying at home is just *one* of the options.

Death is an act of power. Well, Wiccans need not worry: the Goddess is not dismayed when we are bold. "Let there be beauty and *strength*, *power* and compassion, *honor* and humility and mirth and reverence with you," She charges us. These are our natural characteristics and we are allowed to exhibit them! As a rule of thumb, you can bet that Wicca will support any decision that restores power to the people.

Once you know what you think about things, if they're death-things, you should write them down. One way to make your wishes clear is to write a living will. Living wills for Pagans could include instructions about religious observances, which cannot easily be abrogated.

And what if in the meantime you have to decide, to put it bluntly, whether to "unplug" somebody or not? All I can tell you is to trust your instincts. Wicca will support you in that. Consult your usual oracles. Do what you can stand for, "the right thing;" and don't worry about what the people who didn't (have to) stand beside you say.

Meanwhile, if the body's been taken by ambulance from home, hospice, or other site of death, someone will need to arrange to

---

[1] This is a situation in which I would consider it "moral" to not be an organ donor. I think the experience is full of creative potential, and I value the invisible dimensions of life as much as I do the material-visual plane. It seems to me that enough good comes of the really cherished death-at-home experience to balance the loss of the organs. I mention this not to persuade anyone to this opinion, but to affirm the process of account-keeping among our opinions.

move the body from the hospital to a funeral home or cremato-rium. (In cases of home death, if you've been working with a doctor, an autopsy may not be necessary.)

Among other first concerns is whether or not to have the body present at the farewell rites. If you want the body present, you will probably need to choose a funeral home to prepare the body. If you are prepared and your loved one has died at home, you may be able prepare the body yourself. Even if a mortician is involved, you may wish to be part of that process.

One way of facing the Guardians of death, a way our great-grandparents knew, is to help the mortician prepare the body. I did this with both my parents. In my mother's case, the mortician was grossly insensitive, but dressing Mom, both my father and I felt good about attending her right to the end. (It was a very hard and brave thing for my father to do, too.) Her body was, of course, stiff and somewhat contorted, but her face was surprisingly relaxed and looked comfortingly pain-free. (I learned later that there was a wad of cotton, like the ones dentists use, in her mouth to help achieve that effect; no matter, I'm glad it was how I saw her.)

No one who's not a licensed or apprentice embalmer can do the part with the tubes and wires and fluids, but you can, if you find an open-minded funeral director, help to dress the deceased in the special clothes that have been chosen for viewing or for cre-mation or burial, help arrange hair and apply make-up and jewelry and other accessories. (Mom went to the crematorium in her favorite leopard-print pants outfit, and a few months later, Dad went out in his tennis shorts and polo shirt.) You can even be alone with the body to minister to it. There is nothing illegal about this, and if it is something you want or need to do, it is your right.

It can be a daunting prospect, of course—most of us haven't even *seen* a dead body, much less touched one and moved it. Was there a first time you touched a snake, and found out, to your amazement and relief, that they *aren't* slimy and icky like you thought they were? Touching a dead body falls into the same category of experience: expect amazement and relief.

Our culture gives us grotesque, frightening images of dead bodies, and of morticians, too. But participation in the preparation of the body can be tremendously satisfying. It's a challenge, something you have to make yourself do, and an offering—the least we can do for the sake of those we love?

Another decision that needs to be made almost immediately is where to hold the funeral. Many Wiccans and other Pagans are inclined to outdoor sites, but in some situations that precludes having the body present.

Ashes, of course, can be present virtually anywhere. About five pounds of ashes (small bone fragments) are left over from cremation, and that's enough to pretty much fill a container that measures six inches by six inches by ten inches. If you want to keep some ashes in a smaller container, inter some at, say, a family burial site or columbarium (a building with niches where ashes are entombed), and scatter the rest in some place(s) the deceased loved, you will have plenty of material to work with.

If you have made such decisions and preparations well ahead of your time of need, though, and explored the possibilities with a local undertaker, you will be able to accommodate laws and personal and religious preferences much more calmly and creatively, without succumbing to social pressures that might be overwhelming at the last minute. You'll also need to mind details like transportation of the body to and from the funeral site and decide on a "final resting place," which term we use very superficially here to mean a real or designated burial site.

Designated burial site? If the body is cremated and the ashes are scattered over water or in remote woods, it won't be possible for anyone to bring flowers or have a spiritual chat at the grave site. It is very helpful to designate one site, whether it's marked or not, where mourners can come to commune with their loved one whenever they feel the need. When my old cat Angie died, and was buried in our back yard, her grave was where we put flowers for our other belovéd dead, too. Most of them are buried in Portland (Oregon), which is a long way from Tucson (Arizona).

Most commonly, caskets are buried in cemeteries, sometimes called memorial parks. Many of these are affiliated with funeral homes (mortuaries). In most states, mortuaries are required to give you clear and honest information, including their prices for various goods and services, over the phone.

What are the goods and services that funeral homes provide? The goods include the casket itself—and if you want a nice one for viewing[2] prior to or at the funeral rites, many homes will actually rent you one for that purpose, so that you can have the body buried or cremated in something less expensive—and the funeral accessories. Some homes even have burial clothing available. (Please be assured, if you are even a little bit shocked to learn that caskets can be rented, that it is not cold or disrespectful to the deceased to think practically about such matters; nor is it at all "risky" in spiritual terms. The Goddess cares about us and our experiences and our attitudes, and not in proportion to the cost of our send-offs.)

As for services, funeral homes will embalm and prepare a body for cremation, burial, and/or viewing. They'll carry the body in a hearse wherever it needs to go. They can get certified copies of the death certificate, send notices to papers locally and in other places when that's appropriate (you'll have to tell the mortician where else death and/or funeral notices should appear), arrange for flow-

---

[2]I read an article by John Updike in the July 1992 issue of *NewsdigesT,* a Phoenix magazine, about funeral photography. Well, I *love* the idea, and I'll tell you why. In nineteenth-century America, death photography was all the rage; ofttimes the death portrait was the only photo ever taken of a person. It's a link with history, even back to death masks (another custom I'd like to see revived). It's an affirmation of death as a stage of life to be photographed, recorded, and remembered and talked about like other episodes and milestones are recorded. If you like the idea too, but you're not quite up for doing it yourself, talk to one or two professionals. Photographers are artists, and some will be sympathetic to the idea.

ers, and tell callers where to see the body, send donations, or contact relatives.

They'll set up for any graveside services—which could be at a mausoleum (where caskets are entombed in walls or other structures) or a columbarium (where containers of ashes are similarly entombed). They can also take care of music and the clergy's honorarium, and they can arrange for a caterer and reserve a reception site for the after-service gathering; some establishments have their own reception parlors.

You can tell by the goods and services offered what society expects. Being clear about that, you can not only reevaluate your own expectations, but be aware of all the latitude modern expectations of dying, death and funeral doings give our customs and preferences.

Cemetery plots and funerals can be expensive, but there are ways to plan ahead and mitigate those expenses. (Remember that even purely Pagan funerals will cost *something*, even if the accouterments of conventional funerals aren't in your plans.) One way to handle it is to pay for your funeral in advance: "at today's prices," most of the literature says, and this is called a "fixed price funeral trust." Your money goes into a trust with the money of other people who are making the same arrangements. The interest earned on the account (theoretically) offsets inflation. The funeral home you've chosen is allowed to charge a percentage of the total funeral cost for administration and can collect a percentage of the interest each year to maintain the account.

They can't get into the money without proving that they've fulfilled the contract. You can cancel the contract at any time, and if you do, there's a limit on how much of your money the funeral home can keep for their trouble. You can also participate in a "non-fixed-price funeral trust," in which the price of the funeral *isn't* established ahead of time. This means that your survivors may have to supplement the payments you've already made. (Neither of these plans pays for whatever *taxes* there may be on the goods and services you've chosen.)

A third way of dealing with it is to decide what sort of a funeral you want, get an idea how much it will cost, and buy a life insurance policy in that amount, making the funeral home the beneficiary. If you cancel the policy, the designated funeral home is released from any obligation to fulfill your contract, and you may find yourself paying significant penalties. Of course, if you fail to pay the premiums, the policy lapses and you get little or no money back.

Yet another possibility is to establish what's often called a "P.O.D." account—payable on death. The funeral home of your choice will help you with the pre-planning and keep a record of your wishes. You set up a savings account to cover the anticipated expenses, but the price is not fixed. The money in the account is yours, and you can withdraw it at any time, but the funeral home is the beneficiary and the monies will be released to the funeral home at your death.

If you choose this sort of plan, it's up to you to keep the funeral home informed of any changes in your plans, and of the status of your account. You also need to let somebody else know. This plan requires a lot of communication, for the funeral home cannot carry out your wishes if they don't know what your wishes are.

We may hope one day to do business with Pagan funeral homes and burial grounds, to entrust our requiems to groves or covens we know will be thriving when our times come. For now, we must be diplomats and work within the dominant social conventions. If you can avoid it, count yourself lucky. If you or someone you know is terminally ill, then you have time to think about things like which funeral home you'll use, if you want or need to go that route. No matter what arrangements we make, it's just a lot easier to have the major decisions made before you're under pressure to arrange everything in three or four days.

Many cities have memorial societies. As the cover of the Tucson Memorial Society's brochure says, these societies are "dedicated to the promotion of simplicity, dignity and economy in funeral and memorial arrangements through advance planning." They are usually nondenominational. If you want to look at some literature before you get in touch with local people, write to the Continental Association of Funeral and Memorial Societies at 33 University Square, Suite 333, in Madison, Wisconsin, 53715.

Memorial societies generally offer a few options from which you can choose. They often include cremation, direct burial, and an economical funeral that allows for the body's presence at the service. Their prices will be guaranteed for a certain period of time, after which the costs will be higher. If you are a member, you will be advised of such changes. Memorial societies usually have Social Security and Veterans Administration forms on hand, as well as forms to authorize various hospital procedures. Many of them offer worksheets on which you can record details for your family so that they can act with confidence to carry out your wishes.

I'd like to reiterate here that it really puts an extra and unnecessary burden on your survivors if you *don't* leave some indication of what you'd like done after your death. When Canyondancer's mother died, it was only luck that her cousin had an idea where Vivian wanted to be buried, and that idea was from a years-old casual remark. We had to make several other decisions without a clue what her wishes were, and I don't mind telling you it gave me nightmares. Don't make other people do that work for you.

The Requiem Process

Conventionally, funerals themselves happen in churches or funeral home chapels. The casket or some other representation of the deceased is in front of an altar of some kind, usually flanked by flowers. As mourners are ushered in, discreet religious music plays unobtrusively. A cleric opens the service with a prayer and moves into the funeral rite, which is generally read. If the minister didn't know the deceased, someone who did may be asked to speak a eulogy or read favorite Scriptural or other passages. The minister then closes the service and directs the gathered friends and relatives to follow the hearse to the interment site.

A Wiccan requiem is different in all the usual ways that Wiccan worship is different from cowan. If mourners are to proceed to a place of interment, they might leave the Circle through a Door at the Northeast, with one priest/ess staying behind to banish the Circle before joining the others and entering the Circle that's been cast at the burial site.

Further, a Wiccan requiem is different in its thealogy and mood from the dominant norms. We talk about rest and reincarnation, not about eternal commitment to any hell or heaven. Our belief is that death is a reunion with the Goddess, a return to Her womb in anticipation of rebirth, and there is no vengeance in the womb. Her love is unconditional and all-powerful, and trust in it is our natural state, to which death restores us if nothing else has.

How do we compromise with the funeral goods and services commonly available—not to mention their enormous cost, when it seems vaguely sacrilegious to charge at all for burying the dead—without compromising our Traditions and symbolism? How can we express *our* faith without seeming to disrespect other religions' burial customs?

Well, what we're likely to do in public ritual is not going to dismay the mainstream overmuch. One thing we don't have to worry much about is holding the service out of doors. People are familiar enough with graveside services that it doesn't seem strange to be outside, even if there isn't an actual grave nearby—and even if the weather is inclement.

Privately, there are more deeply meaningful things we can do, and the mainstream is even opening a little to some of those. Rich and appropriately deep symbolism attaches to just about any funeral arrangements we make. The important thing is that what happens at our requiems symbolizes our real lives, not what somebody else thought or hoped about our lives.

Do not worry or regret that some of your mourners may have to go out of their way to make the arrangements you want or do something else you ask them to. When it attends a death (or a birth, or a handfasting—Wiccan wedding—come to that), a simple errand can become a Quest. By leaving such errands (or more serious challenges) for your friends, you turn your death into a mythic landscape and their grief into an adventure. That can be your blessing upon them. If someone's funeral task teaches them something they never knew about their loved one, it's *another* blessing.

Our mortality gives us enormous power. Not all of us will have the opportunity to "go out in a blaze of glory," in spectacular rescue or some other heroic act. But we can all use that power to charge the marking of our passage, just as we all bring our strengths to bear on any passage we celebrate, our own or the God's. How different any Wiccan funeral will be from the better-known cowan services will depend almost entirely on the circumstances in which we die. What is the tolerance of the Craft here? What legal restrictions apply? What are the physical opportunities for ritual? What is the ideal?

The ideal Wiccan funeral is, of course, a different thing for each of us, just as the ideal Wiccan life is different in every Witch's mind. Our stories are meant to be different, for if it were just the same for all of us, we'd tire of hearing one another up and down the table at the feasts!

Remember that most people expect a funeral to be mysterious, death being the Major Mystery it is. Only when mourners are expected to do something *other* than be quiet and watch do you need to worry much about explanations. When directions or explanations are necessary, keep them short and simple. Don't apologize: nobody else does. People expect to be inconvenienced by funerals, and more often than not they actually appreciate it, because it assuages much of whatever guilt or loss of control they're feeling.

My mom's memorial service is a case in point. Although neither of my parents were Wiccan, neither of them was Christian, either. My dad proudly told all his friends that his daughter "the minister" was going to conduct Martha's funeral, not realizing that they'd assume I was a Christian minister. Their first surprise was that, though it was February in Oregon, I was barefoot. But they all considered it their obligation to Martha to be open-minded about her funeral rites.

The backdrop was an aging and grimy Soothing Panorama of plastic ferns, complete with what Canyondancer assures me was a dove, and I maintain was a seagull, hanging from the ceiling. I set up an altar-table with bowls of incense, salt, honey, and water. At the beginning of the service I told the assembled mourners that at the end of the service they'd have a chance to bless themselves with the incense smoke, taste a fingertip of salt to acknowledge the bitterness of death, taste a fingertip of honey to acknowledge the sweetness of life, and bless themselves again with the water from which we are all born and reborn. I explained what it all meant.

And at the end of the service, I demonstrated how to do all of these things.

I left the main chapel and went with my dad to stand in the adjacent hall to speak personally with Mom's mourning friends and thank them for coming. Canyondancer and the Explorer followed us first, setting the smoke-salt-honey-and-water example again. I couldn't resist peeking back through the doorway to see how it was going. I nearly dissolved in giggles when it became clear that all the "little old ladies" were getting through the incense, salt, and honey just fine . . . but they were all using the water as a finger-bowl. Lord love them all for finding a way to make the strange Pagan ceremony something they could understand. "Crazy little Martha's" sense of humor was greatly and appropriately honored at her memorial service.

As for casting our Circles, the truth is that funerals tend to distract people, and the religious things that clergy are doing aren't going to provoke much immediate comment even if people are paying close attention. If you are worried about someone's breaking the Circle or doing anything else inappropriate, ask someone to be a Warden and coach mourners who need direction; and include brief instructions in the printed "program," another thing that a funeral home can make available.

If you are including anything original in the printed program, I'd suggest asking to see a proof. I discovered, minutes before Mom's service was to begin, that the printers had left out two lines of the poem we had provided. The omission really gutted the poem, and the funeral home's offer to print new ones a week or two later didn't really help. Neither did the fact that the non-Pagan mourners probably never noticed the error.

In mixed religious relationships, it's not unusual for people to steer clear of each other's religions, each trying to acknowledge the other's privacy and freedom, and in many cases, avoid argument. One consequence of this mutually agreed-upon ignore/ance is that nobody knows what to do for a service when anybody dies. *Wanting* to do something the other person would have liked is beside the point when you don't *know* what the other person wanted. Intent is impotent without information.

If you leave instructions, then the people left behind won't have to chop maplessly through the dark and scary woods when you die. Your people can do what needs to be done and find strength in the knowledge that their efforts *do* fulfill your last wishes.

Adventure teaches us that only by paying attention to our mortality can we hope to survive our encounter with it. If you look at death as an experience that's going to *end* your life, then you're likely to relinquish responsibility and control when you die. If you look at death as an experience that's going to *change* your life, then you're likely to undergo a marvelous transformation when you die, just like a well-prepared kid will probably ace the driver's test.

Typically, the Adventure Tradition gives us this example: if what's happening doesn't look to be all that good for you personally, then consider the good of the community you represent, and if things still don't look very good, then do your best to die inspiringly anyway. This leaves you with a lot to coordinate in your final moments, but having the capacity to make your death experience a creative, cohesive whole for all concerned is both why you're in this predicament in the first place and the only way you will survive to remember it from other incarnations.

It's important for clergy to face their Guardians, confront their own mortality, be able to articulate their beliefs, and be comfortable with the idea that we *do* have to die to be reborn.[1] It's *also* important for Wiccan clergy to resolve any questions in their own

---

[1] I hear a few Boomers talking about not wanting to get old because the old people they remember were frail and fearful. Old age doesn't have to be like that. We have a chance, by our own wills, to bust that lie. You don't have to die young to die well, and 102 doesn't have to be pathetic. (England's late Queen Mother was 101 when she died in 2002, and was "with it," if somewhat physically impaired, till the end.) Very old age used to be taken for granted in heroes. Irish folk hero and demigod Finn MacCool, for instance, passed 200 easily and died heroically! Boomers and Witches both know something about shaping energies. Brave heart: reclaim your whole life, even the end of it.

minds about what is appropriate religiously and what is possible practically, because there may be no time for such "moral" deliberation when coveners or solitaries in our communities come to us for comfort or counsel or requiems.

We are here, we think, to explore, to experience, to see, to imagine, to understand, to learn, to grow. The Universe itself is expanding, and that seems like a pretty clear instruction to us: if as above, so below, and if the Universe is expanding, then so should I be. From every experience we have, we extract as much as we can. We go over the details, comparing them with memories of other experiences, watching for new patterns, wondering what they mean when we see them, guessing, hoping. We pull back and try to see the general trends and how they relate to one another, where the strands of the web are thickest, so to speak.

So when one of us dies we say s/he has gone before us into the Quest—and the Goddess reassures us that beyond death we shall have reunion with those who have gone before. So we wish the traveler interesting challenges, and wish ourselves the same, and our rites are in the *hail, fellow, well met* and *merry meet again* vein, because that is the way of Adventure.

Other Traditions use different metaphors, visualize different landscapes, but we all joust for the same Queen, and we all look forward to riding with the same King in the Wild Hunt. But all these metaphors, all these landscapes, aren't they just pretty fantasies? In my opinion, no more (and overall, less harmfully) than pearly gates and streets paved with gold are fantasies. As long as we remember that we're describing a nonmaterial experience in material terms, they remain and are useful as metaphors.

Lots of these "fantasies" address the confusion of puberty with analogies to being landed into a strange country where you don't know the rules, and you're given outrageously daunting tasks which involve the highest of stakes. Well, the confusion of loss is comparable, and when somebody dies or a dearly held hope is shattered, you can feel equally disoriented.

This is an opportunity to live mythically, to realize that you've landed in the heart of the universal psyche. If you ground and center, you'll find that you *do* know the rules, and you *do* have the "weapons"[2] you'll need on this Quest. Grief—along with fear and anger and confusion—changes your brain chemistry. You don't have to cast a formal Circle to get between the Worlds, because your chemistry will take you there before you know it. If you're a Witch, and maybe even if you're not, you know something about how to behave between the Worlds. It is *not* more than you can handle.

Just as the death of this incarnation's body is not an "end," neither is any gain you might realize from it. In fact it's a legacy, and you can do your loved one much honor in your use of what s/he's left to you, or what comes to you after s/he's died. In other words, your inheritance or incredibly good fortune in death's shadow is not the end of the story, either. It is a *never*-ending story; but that aside, it's not the end of *your* story. It's no more wicked to inherit or otherwise benefit from a death or a loss than it is wicked to save grains of last year's corn and plant them again.

In our rites, we *deliberately* raise energy that is enough to frighten some people. We are not afraid of the dark, not any of the darks; we certainly don't need to be afraid of Life or the power of our own feelings. We know how to ground excessive power, we know how to spin it and shape it and bind it and send it. We might find ourselves manipulated by relatives or other authorities in terms of the physical arrangements we make for deaths and losses, but we need not be bullied so far as our feelings and attitudes go.

Intent is the cornerstone of any magic, including life-magic. Many disadvantages, even severe ones, can be overcome at least to some degree, if our will is intact. The time does come for all of us when our will separates from our body. The release of energy

---

[2]I don't like to use the word *weapons*, really, because I don't mean to imply the pocket grenades or >POOF< potions of Pentagon fantasies and video games. I use it, as many Wiccans do, to mean *magical tools*.

when this happens is intense—more intense than most of what we feel in our incarnate state. It is therefore important to learn to control our intent in the face of any number of distractions. Pain and loss and frustration and incapacity are all distractions. The *Tibetan Book of the Dead* speaks of the minor mandalas that are less bright, less intimidating than the central one to which we're drawn when we die. Less intense, they seem safer, and distract many souls; being thus distracted is one idea of how you get to be a ghost.

Similarly, in this incarnation, pain and failings are distractions from our real callings. There's no punishment, other than the *Gee, I could have had a happier life* sort of realization we speak of making in the Summerland.

While our metaphors oughtn't be misread for exact parallels of life after life, I know that I feel like a real jerk when I get done with a project and realize that there was a much easier way. It's along the lines of trying to make that pouch you see in your head, and eventually getting it the way you want it after several tries. Death is no more "punishment" than that is. And I believe that just as I can do it that easier way next time I make a pouch or a banner or something, I can learn in my next life from the "mistakes" I've made in this one. There need be no question of guilt.

Fortunately, if you are a Wiccan you don't have to rely on any ecclesiastic authority to tell you what you believe about what's happened, or to interpret the meanings of your belief for you. Your clergy—and that includes you—will help you access your own power to understand and deal with what's going on. There are many magics which may help if you are coping with debilitating or life-threatening illness or injury. Furthermore, if you don't see what you need in any of the books you've read, you're not only free, you're *encouraged* to put something together for yourself.

You may find yourself without your motor power, without your usual stamina, without your family, missing this or that or something else. But you are never alone, and you are never without the enormous power of spirit that is our common blood in life.

Much of the guilt we end up feeling for the things that happen to us is learned. People may raise their eyebrows at us if we don't suppress our anger; and we worry that we might lose everybody else we love, too, if they see us screaming or crying or complaining. We've been asked for so long to suppress and deny our feelings precisely *because* they are powerful.

Acting from the power of those feelings, we are formidable and can accomplish much—like the overthrow of oppressive institutions and recovery from oppressive illness. The healing is coming right along, but we are not quite back from the brink of those feelings scaring *us* as well as the material world's powers that be. We can learn not to be scared of ourselves, of our experience, our power. Wicca is helpful. Wicca's thealogy is empowering; and Wicca, being an experiential religion, offers us tangible proof of our own authority in rituals that are powered by our own energy.

When we're in control of our own energy—not in defiance of nature, not by suppressing our feelings or judging and rejecting or denying them, but by "owning" them, as the pop psychologists of the 1970s put it, by facing them and integrating them and thus harnessing their energy and directing it, we are healthier. That's because we humans are *meant* to be in charge of our lives in this way.

Wiccans rehearse death in every Initiation—and that's whether we're being initiated or helping to initiate—and these rehearsals are a little like physical therapy. When someone sustains serious damage to her nervous system, it is often necessary to reprogram the muscles and synapses by recreating the movements of crawling and other pre-ambulatory motions. Initiation rehearses death in the same way, but metaphorically, teaching us to expect rebirth rather than retribution.

Just as there is nothing guilty about a person's needing muscular reprogramming, there is nothing guilty about death or our participation in it. Death is not a failure or a punishment. It is a stage in our life, and our reactions to it, the uses we make of it, are natural. Like everything else about life, death raises energy, and like any other energy, it is ours to deal with as we see fit. *An ye harm none, do as ye will.*

Many of the attitudes we learn to take about our losses come from the idea that there are one or two strikes against us to begin with. If the thought of major losses in your life or the death of your near and dear really devastates you, if you really just can't think about it, then maybe you need to re-evaluate your values.

We're conditioned to accept guilt, and to punish ourselves. Wicca does not equate humanity with sin. Wicca has no concept of sin. I like to quote a priestess, Delia Morgan, who says, "I believe in ignorance and fear, but not evil." Amen. We do not believe our lives to be unworthy. No pain, no gain, Western culture tells us. Nonsense! Pain is a biochemical signal of a problem, not a goal. "Go for the burn" is *not* an appropriate attitude for Witches to take! The idea that we're meant to suffer, meant to accept pain as our lot, is like saying your car's oil light is meant to be on all the time.

Guilt has a place in our lives. When we've done something antithetical—killed or robbed or raped or otherwise power-overed—we *should* feel guilty. It's a natural constraint on our behavior. You know how the monkey in the cage presses the right lever and gets a treat, presses the wrong lever and gets a *zap*, and learns very quickly which lever not to press? The *zap* that guilt feels like teaches us very quickly not to indulge in the behaviors that generate the brain chemistry we call guilt.

The trouble is, our sense of guilt is manipulable because it needs to be imprinted by our culture. It isn't fully developed when we're born because we have to learn our particular tribe's identification of guilt. Spilling a handful of water might not even be noticed by the Clan of the River Bank, but it could well be a capital crime and high blasphemy in the Tribe of the Dry Sands. A lot of guilt-making stimuli are logged in our brains that don't need to be there, that could be safely and constructively deleted. They're left over from environments in which we no longer live—or no longer *choose* to live.

The only way to identify the unnecessary bits of the program is to review them all. In Wiccan terms, this is one way of facing the Guardians. The act of facing the Guardians—symbolizing and manifesting our trust that we won't be possessed or annihilated by the strength of our fears and frailties, or by our tremendous potentials—is widely and deeply and immanently powerful.

The Guardians and facing them is all very real—it's just that the experience occurs in more dimensions than we live in. This makes anything we can say about our experiences between the Worlds metaphorical. Wicca knows full well it's metaphorical—and that's not a criticism or a weakness or an inadequacy. It must be metaphorical—poemogogic, Starhawk calls it—for if it were a cosmology that referred only to Earthly events, it'd be of no use in relating us to the great Beyond,[3] which is a primary function of any religion. (Taking it literally not only generates great misunderstandings and disappointments, but it rather presumptuously imposes limits on the Beyond, I think, by denying there are dimensions we can't literally describe.)

There are no rigid criteria; lateral thinking is encouraged. It's easy to think that the physical is the most important aspect of incarnation, but—and I ask this question as someone who camps in a VW microbus—how often is the car the most important part of your vacation? *Necessary, but not sufficient*, is how they put it in math and logic.

A crippling disease or circumstance is going to take a lot of your energy, yes. It's going to require big changes and little changes and forever changes. You didn't ask for it, you didn't deserve it. You may be angry, you may be scared. And you are a *powerhouse*. You are also God/dess and you have all the authority you need to acknowledge your feelings and draw upon them for inspiration.

---

[3] I do not mean by the "great Beyond" any place outside the Universe. I mean beyond the range of our sensors; there is nothing outside the Universe, and any appearance that there is I take to be an effect of *time*.

Thinking about it magically will help. Here you have this energy. You can't use it to "wish" this condition on anybody else, because you've got the Rede in your face. You can't sit there and sulk for the rest of your life because that would be, at the very least, undignified. You know the Goddess doesn't require sacrifice, so what you're looking at is a trade, an exchange of energy, not anything unilateral: the enactment of a process, not the negotiation of a contract.

Explore that and remember that Wicca holds the inner and communal realms as real and holy as the material ones. Think about your condition as if it were the result of *removing* an obstacle, rather than placing one in your path. What is there you couldn't do before, or didn't, or never thought of, that you can or could do now? Think about that seriously, trustingly. Meditate on it, journey on it. I'm not saying you should be grateful that it happened, whatever it was. I'm saying, Okay, you landed, you're bruised, but here you are. So where and how are you going from here?

Ritualize it. Ground the energy, store it for later, transform it and let your own reclaimed power transform you. *She charges everything She touches, and everything She touches changes*, goes one of the first chants I ever heard.[4] If you *act as if* what's happened to you is a change at Her touch—not Her intention[5]—then you will feel yourself charged. This you may not be able to change, being charged as you have been; but the manner in which the *discharge* proceeds, ah, that is where your power lies. Of course the charge will be renewed, daily if your changes are recent, and it will always be a source of energy to you no matter how many years you put between then and now. And the discharge—how to use the energy of your circumstances—will always be your call.

It is mostly useless to speculate on what we might have done in a previous life to land us here with these problems now. It's of

<hr>

[4] It's Starhawk's.

[5] Life has unconscious aspects; the Goddess being Life, I expect She does, too.

more use, I think, to find—which will, with respect to your future lives, make you the *founder of*—attitudes which will help you refocus within your new environment.

If you feel singled out, don't worry that a Witch is "not supposed to" feel that way. It's energy, and you can work with it. If "singled out" has a bad connotation in your mind, if you need to change that to feeling "chosen," for instance, or "randomly selected," then create a ritual that takes you from an uncomfortable attitude to a self-affirming one. You have to put that ritual together from your own experience, with your own set of symbols, relying on your own sense of direction.

Odin hung for days on Yggdrasil, and lost much—but gained much. Young people throughout the ages have given their limbs and lives for love or loyalty or faith. People don't—can't—always know what they're getting into: sometimes the cloak of destiny is laid upon your shoulders and the path you are to take is pointed out by strangers. A good many magical adventures have been undertaken incognito, too, with princes wearing paupers' clothes, women wearing men's; sometimes immensely powerful people are disguised for this journey, or for part of it, as handicapped or wading through an apparently endless morass of bad luck.

When Wholeness experiences Individuality, there is no preference for form, there is only exultation in the experience of form. The trick is—like realizing you're dreaming without waking up—to realize when your life has taken a mythical turn. It's a difficult thing to realize because very often, circumstances that don't generate death certificates are diminished and trivialized, and we are expected to feel foolish for responding emotionally. Coming when we're already vulnerable, this social response leads us right into self-doubt, not the best tool for working in an already distressed atmosphere.

Not being hierarchical, though, Wicca does not need to devalue the details of our experience. The Goddess does not ask us to sacrifice anything, not even the feelings other gods condemn as selfish. The attention we pay to our own lives and feelings is wor-shipful, because Wiccans "follow the self to find the Self." Neither does Wicca need to rank our experiences at any Morality Head-quarters that tells us what we ought to care about and what we ought not to mind. We accept each other's feelings with respect, insisting only that we each *own* our feelings. We don't "buy it" when somebody tells us that somebody else "made" them feel this way or that way; but we don't challenge anybody's right to recog-nize and express their feelings.

One reason that Wicca doesn't try to censor anybody's feelings is that Wicca doesn't divide the world into the now-conventional categories of Good and Evil. Wiccans don't have to put any feel-ings on the forbidden list, because in our belief and experience there is a place in the Worlds for every feeling. The child's question comes up here: Can wishes hurt people? the child (inner and outer) wants to know. Can unrestricted emotions accidentally work bad magic? the grown-up wonders.

Well, in this context, the answer to both questions is no. When you've just suffered a loss and you're stumbling through the days as best you can, and you find yourself sobbing and banging your fist against the shower wall in sheer anger and frustration at what's happened, no, you're not cursing anybody. Are you acting with intent? Well, probably with the unconscious intent of grounding the huge energies that keep welling up, yes. Are you likely to hurt somebody in the process? Not if you pound on the wall or the floor and not on other people.

Under the stress of any loss, you may well find yourself—or other people—behaving strangely. Providing this is only occasional and doesn't last for a terribly long time, it's okay. Your appetite may change. What you feel like wearing may change. The route by which you drive to work or to the store or to a friend's house or some other favorite place may change. You may want to rearrange the furniture or clean out your closet or go skiing for the first time in your life.

What you feel, and the ideas you have, don't ever need to be condemned. Of course, you can't *do* everything you think about, and you can't act out everything you feel. You *can*, however, acknowledge those feelings and ideas—indeed, you *should*, for several reasons.

One reason to acknowledge the feelings and inspirations that come to you in your experiences of loss is that this acknowledgment, which requires *some* kind of ritual activity, will help to ground you and make it easier for you to function on the ordinary planes. Another reason is that when you are emotionally vulnerable, you need—and I mean *need*, like you need enough sleep and a balanced diet and some cardiovascular exercise—reassurance that you are real and valuable. And all this is whether you've lost your best friend, your job, your dog, your truck, your pay check, your oldest, fondest dream, or Aunt Theadosia's irreplaceable antique silver pin.

Under stress, you begin to wonder whether you have any existence at all beyond your involvement in the crisis. Exhaustion from dealing with the crisis itself and the awkward feelings of your friends can isolate you. If you come home to a darkened house after a full day of coping, you might not even see yourself in the mirror. *Cogito, ergo sum*[6] is all very well and good, unless your cogitations are condemned by social or religious convention. If you've got a world divvied up into "Good" and "Bad," these "selfish" thoughts fall into the "Bad" category. Trouble is, so do you for having them. Well, we all know what happens to "bad" people, and none of us wants to be one, so those "bad" thoughts have got to *go*.

Whoops, now there's *more* trouble, because those thoughts *don't* go away. They're a function of your survival instinct, like sex and thirst and hunger and the fight-or-flee response. Without some-

---

[6]Descartes said it, in Latin; it means, *I think, therefore I am.* And it is pronounced *coe*-ghee-toe *uhr*-go *sum.*

thing being dreadfully wrong, organically or psychologically, you
can't stop being selfish any more than you can stop reactions to
loud noises. In conventional terms, this means that, ultimately,
you've got to put *yourself* in the "Bad" category. Not quite the sort
of encouragement you need to get through rough times.

Wicca *does* offer some encouragement, though. Wicca says *Thou
art God/dess*. You and all your thoughts and feelings. Wiccans are
not expected to offer sacrifice, not required to kill anything, not
even thoughts or feelings. And while, yes, of course, we have to
impose some limits on how we *act*, we have free reign to express
ourselves symbolically in ritual.

Wicca works with energy, tuning individuals to each other until
we become a group, even across time and distance, like the group
of strings on a guitar that give the instrument a much wider and
more complex range than any string by itself has. Wicca's structure,
where it exists, is communal, family-like, and we all have the
opportunity to draw upon the group's energy when ours wanes.
This means that we can become physically as well as psychically
aware that we are not alone, that our energy *is* part of a larger,
deeper resource, and that we have access to that resource. The
exchange of energy that takes place in Circle, in any rite, symbolizes and reminds us of the universal cycles: *as above, so below.*

You can never tell, when you're working through a loss of any
kind, when you will need to rest, when you will be overcome,
when you will feel strong; most people are lucky to recognize
their feelings when they're going through a crisis, much less pre-
dict them or plan ahead to accommodate them. When those vulnerable moments come it's awfully nice to trust a faith that affirms
you just the way you are, a faith that calls you holy even when you
feel (like you're) horrible.

To get a plant out of a seed, you have to endure the *death* of the
seed. But do you mourn? No, you rejoice. The seed's death, you
realize, is really the transformation you've been waiting for, the
conversion of seed into sprout. You welcome the death of the seed

because it means the creation of the sprout. And then those first little leaves fall off—they die—and do we mourn the cotyledons, those little practice leaves that seeds put out to get oriented toward the light? No, we don't. We pay attention to the unfurling "real" leaves and we are pleased with the progress of our plant.

And when we have to thin the bed of seedlings, and we take the fading lower leaves off the plant so that more of its energy can nourish the newer leaves, do we weep for the discarded seedlings? Do we keen over the yellowed leaves that we remove? No, not generally, we don't. We acknowledge that this is part of life, that the life-force of the seedlings lost to the thinning process will be recycled and that the dead leaves served their purpose and will serve the same purpose differently now, as mulch.

Admitting that most of us get much closer emotionally to people than to plants, we're very much less sensible about people's deaths than we need to be. (We could do with being more sensitive to the losses we all suffer with the deaths of so many plants in the world, come to that.) Every birth and death and all growth change this world forever. Every loss and gain, every opinion and idea, is important. That things will change is inevitable. The question is whether we can and will pay enough attention to the patterns to be able to weave our lives into them well and skillfully, with some sense of art.

There's no question that we can do this. We certainly have the capacity: our opposable thumbs and our cerebral cortex give us the ability. What's uncertain these days is our will. Our will is infirm because we have been brought up to mistrust ourselves. Wicca "preaches" *perfect love and perfect trust*, and most of the time we take that to mean perfect love for and perfect trust in the Gods, or our brother and sister Witches; but it's about loving and trusting our own selves, too. We are all God/dess.

I know for a fact that when we are honest with each other, person-to-person, straightforward without any social artifice, truly respectful of each other, really hearing each other, really accepting each other's individuality, touching on all our levels, we're happier. When our relationships are like that, death is easier to bear: the sadness isn't less, but the guilt is, and so is the regret.

Laying our fears down as an offering—laying them aside as the Goddess laid Her robes and jewels aside when She descended to meet Death—we find that a Door opens to us. Overcoming any fears we find in our griefs can be much like overcoming our fear of the sword's challenge at Initiation. It is a question of priorities. We suffer many losses, individually and culturally. My own feeling is that the old labor slogan DON'T MOURN, ORGANIZE is right on in a lot of cases. I think it's right on for the loss of the rainforests and other habitats, for instance, and for the animals and weather systems and other bits of Gaia that live in them.

In this respect, another loss we sometimes choose to suffer is that of our own potential. When we say that we "can't live without" someone, or worry about catching AIDS from the ordinary intimacies of friendship, when we can't imagine ever finding another job, we are proceeding from the mistaken premise that (my apologies to John Donne) every man is an island.

The bell still tolls for us. Our range of alternatives becomes narrower and narrower—physically, as we dismantle our ecosystems, and spiritually, as we blind ourselves even to the fact that we are a part of the Whole. This is a loss harder to bear than death. In fact, it is unbearable: nothing about us, nothing in us is designed or intended to be unaware of belonging to the Universe. This being an unbearable loss, we need not accept it: we are within our rights, our natural rights—indeed, I think we are under a natural obligation—to demand that the culture change to accommodate life. As we will, so mote it be.

CONCLUSION

Death has not always been the supernaturally frightening Hollywood specter of horror movies. Nor have humans "entertained" a nervously comic image of death through most of our life on this planet. Death was once respected as an important aspect of life, as a restful complement to the activity of life on the physical plane.

Our ancestors, living closer to nature, did not fear death because they did not face it alone. (Certainly we can imagine a lone hunter or gatherer, far from camp, taken out by an animal's single swipe or gore; but that's not the kind of "alone" I mean.) Yes, they went through the door one by one as we do today, but they did not approach death alone; neither did they expect fierce judgment or an unchanging afterlife. They expected—as Wiccans do today—to be held in the loving, healing arms of Mother Earth and to be reborn to their tribes and communities.

Witches' Samhain feasts, generation-and-dimension spanning family reunions that they are, recall this expectation, and so does Wiccan thealogy generally. Beyond death, the Goddess promises us "peace, freedom and reunion," and She asks naught of sacrifice.

In many Wiccan Traditions, Initiates are reminded in every Degree that "to be reborn, you must die." And in our individual experiences, we face any number of "deaths" through which we are reborn, stronger and wiser. It is natural for us to trust that we will be reborn stronger and wiser from the deaths of the bodies we currently occupy, too.

Wiccan and cowan alike, though, most of us do not live "natural" lives. Instead, we are walled away from each other, fenced off, and threatened with social and economic failure if we resist the compartmentalization modern Western culture calls "civilized" and "sophisticated." Yet for all our technological advances, we are still at the mercy of the elements: and because we show each other so little mercy, there is little mercy in the world for the Three-fold Law to return to us.

But *as we will, so mote it be*, so all of this can change. Indeed, change is the way of the Worlds, so all of this *will* change, and the only questions, really, are how attentive to change we will be and how fully we will choose to participate in it. Humanity is said to be the only species capable of consciously influencing its own evolution. Maybe; maybe not. What is clear is that we are the only species that has presumed so broadly to influence *other* people's evolution (fur people and fin people and feather people and rock people and plant people, etc.).

Is there a place by the gas or electric heaters, too often our only hearths now, for perfect love and perfect trust? Well, *sure* there is. The thing is, we can still trust the Goddess. So what if our culture has wandered off down a dead-end track? I've done that myself in the woods—I've even wandered into the wrong room in my *house* looking for something! It is the nature of life to experiment, to explore, and it is the nature of exploration to be, sometimes, dangerous. That old saw, *while there's life, there's hope*, is *true*; and we would add, while there's *death* there's hope.

While there's death, there's hope? Yes! Because death is *not* a finality, it's a prelude, a prelude to rebirth. I cannot promise that humanity will not make Earth uninhabitable for itself, but I do believe that *life* will survive. I am a Witch. I believe that in the long term "it" mote be as I will, and it is my will to live, live beyond my tenth decade in this life and through many more lives after that. I must therefore believe (and *do*, wholeheartedly and with a confidence that is as basic to me as my bones and blood) that we will not destroy our home here.

I never expected to see the "death" of the Berlin Wall or the Soviet Union, but we *did* see those deaths, and they were in the service of life. You have seen deaths, too, that you didn't expect to witness, and some of them have been "in the service," too, as you will know if you think back on your life.

Death need not frighten any of us. It saddens us, to be sure; but without our sadnesses, we are joyless. Any psychologist will tell you that if you try to suppress any feeling, you suppress all feeling. Any biologist, for that matter, will tell you that if nothing dies, we're in big trouble. (And a powerful story I heard once from somebody else's Book of Shadows reminds us that, absent death, we are not yet without injury and disease.) Just as any real physical escape from death would wreak terrible and eventually unbearable meaninglessness upon our lives, our symbolic escapes from death wreak pan-dimensional havoc. We are insular, fearful and psychotic, uncivilized in the light of day and scared of the dark. Let's try again.

In science fiction, a genre enjoyed by many Wiccans, one of the top ten rules for dealing with New Experience and Phenomena has got to be, *accelerate directly toward the center*. That's because the power of an Individual experience comes from the core, like engine power on starships. You must meet these phenomena as an equal if you hope to survive: not necessarily meet them with equal armament or technology, but with equal spirit. And to borrow from sci-fi further: if you think the Experience or Phenomenon is probably going to kill you anyway, then you *really* assert yourself.

Well, because science fiction tends toward adventure, and is an heir of the mythos, the guidelines we can derive from it are often delightfully appropriate. *Accelerate directly toward the center* translates easily to advice for many circumstances. *Confront the issues directly. Cut to the chase.* From one version[1] of the Charge, *Keep pure your highest ideal; strive ever toward it, and let naught stop you or turn you aside.*

From my mundane life I've derived some rules, too, but they're much more specific, like *never marry anybody you can't see in a mirror.* Mundane mottos are more specific because our waking consciousness lives have become very specialized. There are not as many liberal arts majors or GPs as there used to be. A lot of our mundane rules are *thou shalt not*s, whereas myth's rules tend to be *thou shalt*ish.

Not all of us now, and not all of us for thousands and thousands of years, can live our mundane lives mythically. Canyondancer and I have dreamed of wandering the land in our Volkswagen camper. It would be our palfrey, and the whole North American continent would be our enchanted Questing Wood; and who knows what manner of Knights and Witches we'd meet! But for now, we must be content to think of our life as *standing for* our ideal. That means stretching it. The grocery store becomes the herb-lined forest path, the office or the volunteer project's deadline becomes the duty of state that a monarch must do when s/he'd rather be wandering the land in a Volkswagen palfrey (so to speak). It means noticing how the different cultures PBS and cable channels show us are similar and how they're different. It means imagining the ways your life could change, imagining what it would be like to live other lives, walk in other landscapes.

Then again, if you don't live where there are grocery stores, you've got to provide your own food, and maybe you have to make your own clothes. Maybe you like to! In fact, lots of people do like to make their own, because it is restorative of our original relationship with the rest of life, and with the Mother, and of our

---

[1]Farrar, *A Witches Bible Compleat*, app. B.

perspective of ourselves as God/dess. Doing it yourself is almost always harder, and almost always worth it. Doing it yourself fosters an attitude, a confidence, a knowledge that threatens the status quo, sometimes overtly. It is in the interest of those who profit by the status quo to maintain it. The status quo divides up the world into "us" and "them," and you know the rest. Everything else gets divided up, and death ends up being captain of the Bad team.

In cooperative human experience, death is but a door; in neo-Pagan experience, we understand that personally, through mythic rites. Wicca is initiatory, and Initiation is a deliberate confrontation of death. Every Initiate, therefore, has the personal experience of going through the Door of Death and coming back through the Door of Rebirth. Such a person can be difficult to subjugate. If you want to subjugate such a person, you'll first have to change this perception of death. One way to do that is to threaten harsh judgments, condemnations, and eternal punishment. If you corroborate that by imposing frightening, painful deaths, you're quite likely to be convincing.

In the Burning Times[2] this was accomplished on the rack and with other truly horrific tortures. These days it's mostly economic and less often fatal; but lots of us are still scared enough by life to be convinced that death is horrible. We're scared to die, scared of the punishments that await us. At the same time, Wiccans profess a different faith. Few of us, yet, have had many opportunities to tread the path that passes the Well and the Cedar. We have been brought up on fear and punishment (and fear *of* punishment); self-doubt and disconnectedness condition our response patterns for fright and anxiety, which can *keep* us out of control. Out of our own control, that is.

Not every Wiccan is in control of his attitude toward death, but Wicca encourages us to repattern our responses and to dis-

---

[2]Roughly the 1300s to the 1600s, although people were murdered (or "executed," or "purified") for various heresies before and after those specific dates.

cover our own resources and our own inner wisdom. Wicca is not about *power-over*, so none of our thealogy is oppressive. The underlying assumption is that unless *we're* healthy, the rest of the planet isn't, either. *As above, so below:* if the rainforests or the savannahs or the mountain jungles where the gorillas live aren't healthy, nor the gorillas themselves nor the northern spotted owls, the rest of the planet isn't, either.

The most reverent, Gods-pleasing thing we can do is restore ourselves to a sense of community, not only with the rest of life on this Earth, but with the life everywhere, the universe, and everything. We need to restore an expectation that from Individuality we will achieve Wholeness, and thence, Individuality again. Wicca does not deny or belittle our belonging to the cycle of rebirth, and Wicca does not direct us toward *release* from the cycle of rebirth. Wicca teaches that the cycle of rebirth *is*, and is the nature of the cosmos. To participate in it is . . . natural, and pressed, most Wiccans would call it "good," and not a condition from which we want release or require salvation.

Most Wiccans, at least those that I know and read, would disagree that our mundane physical lives are illusory or delusory. Certainly the mundane physical is not the *only* plane on which life . . . lives, but neither is it *less* significant than any of the others. With this understanding, death is no longer a passage to fear, although it's definitely appropriate to be nervous and excited, the way you are before any Initiation. When we undertake that particular Initiation, we must still remember the passwords: *perfect love and perfect trust*, for in the Cosmic Circle we enter at death, our initiators are the Gods themselves.

Now, we trust our priest/esses on this plane not to let us come all the way to the northeast Door unless they think we are ready to make the assay, so I think it's alright to trust that we don't have to die unready to make the assay, either. We work for the Initiations we take on this plane, and similarly we should work toward the final Initiation we'll take in this incarnation.

One of the first Initiations in which I took part saw a young priest surprised with a blanket thrown over his head while we sat by the campfire one Beltane. He knew his priestess had agreed to his request for Initiation, but he hadn't known when to expect it. Just so, we all know we'll die, because we live. We just don't know exactly when the Goddess's blanket will fall over our heads. It's best to keep the passwords in mind at all times.

That doesn't mean that to prepare for death we need to take up death-defying hobbies, although one Witch's defiance may be another's afternoon tea. It does mean taking the journey to the Inner Door, and through it, to your own Underworld, your own Summerland, your own Waste Land,[3] and back again. Your journey to the universal Summerland could start five minutes from now; maybe your body won't die for another 75 or 80 years.

Wicca is *about* change, about participating in the changes we undergo. "Magic is the art of changing consciousness at will," Dion Fortune said. Death is the ultimate change of consciousness (*ultimate* being a relative term, of course). Does that mean we're supposed to want to die? Nope. It means we need to apply our will to our experience of death as we do to our experience of life. Death isn't the end of our contribution, it's *part* of our contribution, like rebirth.

Death is not naturally *not* part of our lives. Same as we do with other things that "hang us up," we can confront the attitudes and assumptions about death that bother us. What many of us learned about death when we were growing up is not what we believe now and not what we would teach our children or apprentices. Yet we can't find out whether what we "think" or "believe" or "feel" about death makes sense to us unless we *look* at our attitudes and assumptions.

---

[3] It's a reference to T. S. Eliot's poem, of course, but also to Joseph Campbell's discussion (in *Creative Mythology*) of Eliot, Yeats, Freud, and a charming assortment of mediaeval philosophers who say that we live in a wasteland when we have abandoned our faith.

If some custom or belief we take for granted is disturbing, why? What rules or dogma drives our judgment? Are they all rules or principles we affirm in our lives? Can some of them be discarded? Where did we learn these things? Do we really agree with everything we've been taught about death? Does it jibe with our experience? Our answers are our own, of course. Not *everything* we've got from non-Pagans is horrible, and it's not as though confronting our feelings has to be a complete rejection of what our families taught us. The process we recommend is, rather, one of examination and acknowledgment. Here is a visualization to try:

Settle yourself comfortably so you feel secure. Imagine a warmly lit staircase with white-washed plaster walls, winding pleasantly to an attic with big, south-facing windows. It's not at all ominous, and it's a wonderful sunny day and you can hear songbirds in the trees outside. This attic is not cramped, and you make yourself comfortable sitting on a floor pillow in front of an old trunk. Opening it, you're aware of wonderful scents—lavender, roses, maybe a little cinnamon. It reminds you of warm, friendly times in your past.

Inside there's a jumble of old papers, curled at the edges and yellowed, some of them quite brittle. The writing on many of them has faded and the ink looks old. You pull out a handful and start to read them. You realize that what you are reading are the definitions, the descriptions, the warnings and witticisms you heard about death while you were growing up, at home, at school, at camp, in the service, at work, in church. As you peer at the old-fashioned writing and the dimming words, sound them out in your mind, as if they were poems. Remembering how they were said, you think about what they mean.

Take two or three of them to the windows to examine them in the sunlight. There in the bright beams, think about which ones of these worn old sayings you might tape to the refrigerator. With any saying(s) you like or feel a need to deal with, come back down the staircase and find yourself once again in the here and now. Take some deep breaths, and when you're grounded again, go find a nice piece of paper and write that saying or idea down and tape it to your refrigerator. Leave it there for a week, and make notes in your journal as thoughts about it occur to you. Then take the saying down and either keep it or burn it.

If you do this every now and again for a year or so, you'll have sorted through that trunk and it will have been a pretty painless—which is not to say never sorrowful—accomplishment of a pretty important thing to understand: that the conventional reports of death are greatly exaggerated.

What all of us need to understand—what I hope this book has helped to make clear and real—is that death has always been sad, but it *hasn't* always been frightening. And though it will always be sad, it doesn't ever have to be scary again.

Some Things to Think About

When you copy the checklist that follows, leave lots of lines and spaces to add your own thoughts, make your own sketches. We are all always growing, and while we are, no list can ever be complete. This is a starting point.

Things to Think About

Final disposition

Preparation of body

add herbs

dress body

spend time alone with body

anoint

photographs[1]

death mask

Cremation

direct

after service

in coffin

in container

shrouded

robed

skyclad

other clothes

---

[1]Some people think the idea is cool, some think it's gross. Respect each other. If you don't want to take pix, don't; but don't be too quick about forbidding other people to. (In the nineteenth century, death photos were all the rage because dead people were among the few who could stay still long enough for the old-fashioned photo process.)

Disposition of ashes
    inter   share
    scatter   use in ritual
    keep
Burial (body or ashes)
    direct
    after viewing
    after service
        open casket
        closed casket
            purchase casket
            rent casket
Site or designated site

Disposition of Tools

Buried/cremated with
Separately committed to Earth/Fire
Passed on
Left in trust for future lives
Left to a collection (coven, museum)

BoS	Box
Athame	(Other items)
Chalice	Correspondence
Pentacle	Compositions
Staff	Collections
Sword	

Ritual

Time of day/night	Altar placement
Site	Altar layout
Chants	Priest/esses
Instrumental music	Eulogy
Movement/dance	Rites

Circle layout and logistics
Adjournment to second site
Adjournment to reception
Robed?
Printed "orders of service" (including words to chants)
Guest book

Remembrances

Flowers or donations sent where? (local charities or neo-Pagan groups, national neo-Pagan groups and sanctuaries? We like to donate the flowers, if there were any at the service, to local hospitals or nursing homes.)
Photos or other memorabilia on view? (You can make a poster-board, or just set a few things out. We had a booklet of my dad's short stories out for people to read at his service, and his fishing pole and tennis racket.)
Grave goods
    what goods?
    contributed by whom?

Reception following services

Site of reception
    someone's house
    a rented place
    a park or grove (do you need reservations?)
Music
Food (this will depend on time of day, season, and other circumstances; it can be anything from nuts and mints to a smorgasbord sort of meal, and it would be nice to include some of your loved one's favorite foods, too.)
    catering
    ask people to bake for you
    set aside time to do some baking yourself

Table settings
  plates
  cups or glasses
  napkins
  utensils/serving pieces
  serving dishes
  tablecloth or mats

Someone to be in charge other than the bereaved
  Who to invite
  Transportation
    who needs rides
    parking
    maps
  Activities
    further ritual
    charm-making
    planting something
    preparing a community donation

Mundane Tasks
  Who needs to be notified?
    employer
    relatives
    friends
    out-of-town correspondents
    insurance companies (including auto and
      homeowners/renters—are there refunds due?)
    subscriptions (refund?)
  How many (certified?) copies of the death certificate will
    you need?
  What will you say to people who call and don't know?
  Are there kids? Who is taking care of them?

Who will take care of the "calling all debtors" notice in the
    paper?
Cancel credit cards and ask for final statements
Call the utilities
Sell the house, notify the landlord, deal with the furniture
    and clothes
Keep track of who sends food, flowers, donations and write
    thank you notes
Decide how many and which "death traditions" you might
    want to keep

Wakes have never really gone out of style. People do still put
pennies on the eyes—or in the pockets—of the dearly deceased.
(In fact, found pennies, often called "pennies from heaven," are
frequently taken as a Sign from the loved one that s/he is "okay"
after death.) People and pets are buried with all manner of grave
goods and mementos. Flowers on the grave (or on the water) is an
ancient tribute, too. Of course, many ethnic groups, geographical
regions, and clans or families have their own traditions. If none
occur to you off-hand, check your local library.

I like the idea of a funeral wreath. I like it so well that I made
one—a large grapevine wreath, decorated with crêpe paper or
cloth ribbons and with symbols of the deceased's life—for each
of my parents. Our "camping contingent" likes the idea so well
that we take one to every Samhain camp now and tuck notes to
our belovéd dead into it. After the ritual, we burn it, and the
smoke carries our messages to the other realms.

I've heard the arguments against wearing black to funerals and
to mourn, and I think it's fine for people to wear red or purple or
whatever channels mourning energy for them. The important
thing is that we acknowledge death having an impact on us. As it
is, we try to just go on, aim to act like nothing has happened; we
expect to be praised and affirmed for taking it all in stride, for
taking it well. Ha!

Any experience of death changes our brain chemistry. Brain chemistry being our electrochemical interface between energy and matter, we would do well to pay attention to changes in it, even as we keep an eye on the temperature gauge in the car. The question isn't *whether* death affects us, it's *how* it will affect us. The specifically Wiccan questions are how we will choose to perceive the energies of death, and how we will direct them. As it nearly always does, it comes down again to our vision of the Whole time-life-space thing, our experience of Maiden, Mother and Crone, and our experience of ourselves, the God.

That we understand the workings of the Worlds in terms of energies upon which our energy can have an effect (the surfing analogies take a lot of flak, but they're legitimate anyway) is one of the bits that distinguishes Wicca from other religions. That we fathom the practical and philosophical consequences of that understanding differently is the source of our diversity. Being aware of the significance of our choices, of the power inherent in making deliberate symbolic choices, is our strength, our authority.

So it *is* important to think about how you'll express your grief. It's important to face your grief squarely enough to know what your feelings are, and from that energy conjure a symbolic act—a color choice, an idea for a wake, commitment to a cause, a change of habit for a year, something(s) that represent(s) both mourning of death and affirmation of life. It is just this transition, I think, over which Wicca gives us power. Let us no longer be intimidated by doctrine we know to be false! Wear any color you like to the funeral, but wear it mythically.

BEYOND DEATH, I GIVE YOU

PEACE

FREEDOM

AND REUNION.

BLESSÉD BE

Farewell, I Bid You
(on Your Way to Summerland)

Music and lyrics by Ashleen O'Gaea

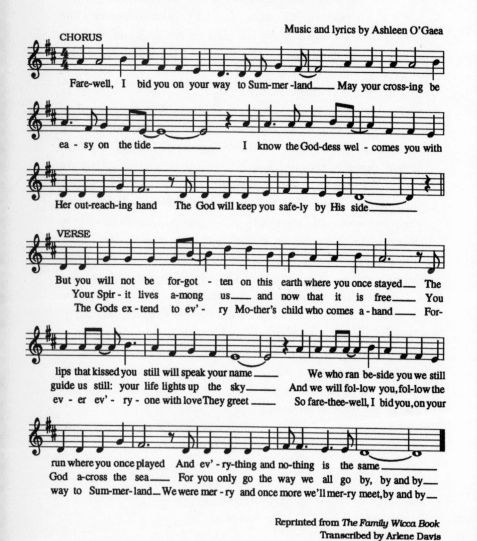

CHORUS

Fare-well, I bid you on your way to Sum-mer-land___ May your cross-ing be

ea - sy on the tide_____ I know the God-dess wel - comes you with

Her out-reach-ing hand The God will keep you safe-ly by His side___

VERSE

But you will not be for-got - ten on this earth where you once stayed___ The
Your Spir - it lives a-mong us___ and now that it is free___ You
The Gods ex - tend to ev' - ry Mo-ther's child who comes a - hand___ For-

lips that kissed you still will speak your name____ We who ran be-side you we still
guide us still: your life lights up the sky____ And we will fol-low you, fol-low the
ev - er ev' - ry - one with love They greet ____ So fare-thee-well, I bid you, on your

run where you once played And ev' - ry-thing and no-thing is the same_____
God a-cross the sea___ For you only go the way we all go by, by and by___
way to Sum-mer-land___ We were mer - ry and once more we'll mer-ry meet, by and by___

Reprinted from *The Family Wicca Book*
Transcribed by Arlene Davis

Glossary

Adventure is the name we give to the Western literary/cultural tradition that guides us in Campsight, and which also influences the secular culture. We come from King Arthur and the Norman Invasion and Robin Hood; the heritage can be extended farther back, of course. It's not that we take our *rites* from the Arthurian legends, it's that we take our broad attitudes and expectations and relationships to honor from those stories and others like them.

As above, so below is a Wiccan way of saying that natural laws apply universally and that our interconnectedness makes all realms metaphors for one another.

The **astral** is a name for the planes or dimensions of reality that exist beyond the realm of ordinary sight and measurement. Some of these are personal and some are universal. (See **the inner**.)

An **athame** (uh-*thah*-may or *ah*-thah-may) is a ritual knife, usually but not always double-edged, used to cast Circles and for other magical purposes; never used as a weapon.

Beta endorphins are wonderful little brain chemicals that alter, and thus mitigate, your experience of pain.

Between the Worlds is a symbolic place at the center of the universe. Wiccans know that the physical world is not the only world in which we live, that there are other realms and dimensions. The Underworld, the Spirit World, and other aspects of the astral are between the Worlds; so can be emotional and psychological realms. In Circle or meditation we are between the

189

Worlds, in a sacred space where the physical and the potential interface, and where our rites and magic can draw upon their combined energies.

Beyond the veil means beyond what we can see, hear, taste, touch, or know intellectually. Ghosts and the vastness of the universe are both beyond the veil. At Samhain—Halloween—we say the veil between the Worlds is thin. This means that it's difficult to distinguish between life and death, so everything can be part of either, or both. "Parting the veil" is a reference to perception beyond the distinction between life and death.

A **Book of Shadows** is a hand-written book of rituals, spells, charms, chants, journal entries, meditations, etc., kept by every Witch. Traditionally black-covered, the "B.O.S." is not shown to the uninitiated.

Boomers are "baby boomers," that enormous and enormously powerful generation born between 1946 and 1964.

Burial vaults are the containers that hold a coffin that's going to be interred in the earth. A vault or liner is usually required so that the grave won't collapse.

The **Burning Times** is another name for the Inquisition. Our lore tells us that nine million Europeans were burned to death because they wouldn't knuckle under to the Catholic Church/state.

Cash advance items are those things a funeral director pays for on behalf of the bereaved family, and things for which the family has to reimburse the director. We're talking about flowers, newspaper announcements, copies of the death certificate, etc.

Caskets can be made of pressboard, wood, or metal; these are the containers in which a body is buried in the earth. If you can find the proverbial "plain pine box," you're lucky.

Chalcedony (kal-*sid*-uh-knee) is a kind of quartz, milky, waxy-shiny and sometimes tinged gold or red with various ores.

Chants are rhythmic, repetitive, and sometimes rhyming phrases voiced in a sing-song way. They can consist of one word intoned over and over, with assorted variations; of several words or sounds repeated in any number of patterns; and they can be sung as rounds. They're meant to put you into a light trance, and so they will if you give them a chance, which means sounding them for five minutes or longer.

The **Charge of the Goddess** is one of the best-loved pieces of Wiccan liturgical material, recomposed by Doreen Valiente for Gerald Gardner. Adapted by many traditions of the Craft, the Charge is instruction and direction, encouragement, promise, enchantment, and mystery.

A **Circle** is a ritually dedicated sacred space where Wiccans' (and some other neo-Pagans') rites are conducted "between the Worlds." Marked at least by psychic energy and the Priestess's sword or athame, the circumference also supports Quarter candles at the compass points. A Circle may be marked with stones, more candles, and drawn lines, or with an embroidered or painted mat. Once cast, a Circle may not be entered or left until a door, quickly resealed, is ritually cut. The psychic energy of a Circle is always grounded at the close of ritual and celebration, but the physical demarcations may be left in place if the Circle is on safe private property. When we spell circle with a small c, we mean our circle of family or friends or the wider Wiccan or Pagan community, according to context.

The **collective unconscious** is the race memory, usually considered as the race memory of human beings; but in *King, Warrior, Magician, Lover,* Robert Moore and Douglas Gillette suggest that it's wider than that, composed of the race memories and increasing experience of *all* life forms, and of course that makes complete sense. It's another way of conceiving the astral, Summerland, the Underworld; it has many names and faces.

Columbariums are buildings full of niches to hold cremation urns. They can look a lot like the insides of post offices, with rows of little boxes, but there are more flowers, bigger windows, and better views.

A **container** is what they call the pressboard box in which a body is cremated.

Cotyledons (cottle-*lee*-dons) are the first little orienting leaves a plant puts up when it's just coming up. They fall off shortly and conventional leaves start growing.

A **coven** (*cuh*-vun) is traditionally composed of six couples and a leader; now, a coven can contain anywhere from 3 to 15 Witches. Covens are the basic unit of Craft organization and are autonomous, led by a priest/ess who is "first among equals." Many covens are quite family-like.

Cowan (*cow*-un) means simply *not Wiccan* or *not neo-Pagan*. It's mostly used by Wiccan writers, but some Witches of other traditions use it too.

Cremains are what's left when a body is cremated. On the average, cremains weigh about five pounds and look like the garden substance vermiculite, only chalkier.

Cremation is the process by which a body is reduced to small bone fragments, which may or may not then be pulverized. Cremation occurs at about 2500°F which, just for the record, is *many* times hotter than a hearth- or campfire ever gets.

A **crematory** is the building where bodies are cremated. The furnace is called a retort.

Death in the service of life is any natural or willing death that contributes to the life of the group (tribe, species, planet, etc.). Predation and aging and seed-cycles in the wild, death in childbirth, rescue and defense in human culture are examples of death in the service of life. Not (or not necessarily) in the service of life are deaths by war, murder, execution, for sport, or as the result of cruelty or individual or institutional psychopathy.

Deathing is the process of sitting with a dying person and performing rituals to make his or her dying easier; also the name of a book written by Anya Foos-Graber.

The **Descent** is the short name of a story/rite about the Goddess's descent into the Underworld to confront Death.

Deosil is a Craft term for Sunwise (clockwise) movement.

A **designated burial site** is a place where a body or ashes may or may not be buried, but where mourners can go to pay their respects to someone who may have died distantly in time or space. There may be more than one designated burial site for an individual.

Desire, the end of all is what we attain in the Goddess when we die. In this context, desire is the basic set of mortal needs and senses by which we're aware of being Individual. The end of it occurs when in death or shamanistic experience your consciousness spreads beyond Individuality to Wholeness, which is Goddess.

Direct burial occurs as soon as the body has been moved from the site of death to the funeral home, put in a casket, and taken to the burial site. This eliminates public viewing or graveside services.

Direct cremation is just like direct burial, except that the body's not interred, it's cremated, without any public viewing.

The **disposition** of a body is what is done with it as soon as the coroner has released it. Burial and cremation are examples of dispositions; so is donation of the body to a research facility.

Earth burial is the funeral industry's term for a burial in the ground.

Embalming is a process by which a body is treated with chemicals so as to temporarily preserve it, as for viewing before or during a funeral service or for transportation to a distant funeral or burial site.

Entombment is the placement of a body above the ground, in a casket, in a mausoleum. A lot of English kings were entombed, and while most of us can't afford that much space in a cemetery or to build the classic above-ground tomb, there are facilities where a casket can be entombed in much the same way that an urn of ashes is stored in a niche. The niche for a coffin is considerably larger.

Esbats are meetings scheduled by the Moon. Most Witches meet on the full Moon, many on the new (dark) Moon, and some on the quarter Moons as well.

A **funeral director** can also be called a **mortician**; s/he's the one in charge of preparing the body for disposition. States test and license funeral directors and other mortuary staff by different standards, and it's a good idea to get in touch with your state's Board of Funeral Directors to find out how it's organized where you live.

A **garter** is a symbol of priestesshood and coven leadership. One place we still see it in use as a symbol of special position is in weddings, where the bride's display of it reinforces her new authority as the mistress (of the manor). Some Wiccan traditions use them today, with the number of buckles attesting to the number of "daughter covens" that have "hived off" from the High Priestess's.

The Gates is a metaphorical reference to the passage from life to death and back again. Upon death, a person passes through the Gates. In a near-death experience or in life-changing crises, or in ritual or therapy, one can face the Guardian of the Gates.

The **God** is a personification of an aspect of life's energy, the Wiccan image of all that dies and is reborn. He is often depicted with antlers or horns to represent the game that falls to the hunter so the tribe can live. He is also seen as the Green Man, representing the grain and other plants that die in the annual harvest so that life can continue.

The **Goddess** is a personification of another aspect of life's energy, the Wiccan image of all that is generative and eternal, the principle by which death becomes life again. Mother Earth, Mother Nature; Maiden, Mother, Crone. Her awareness is the source of our humanity; we are the vehicle of Her awareness. (See also **thealogy**.)

Grave goods are a symbolic and magical collection of memorabilia, gifts, and supplies for someone who has died, a pouch or packet of ritual credentials and tools for the spirit world. The goods themselves are buried or cremated with the deceased; their psychic energy equips the journeying soul.

Grave liners are made of steel or concrete and they're used to keep the sides of the grave from collapsing on the coffin. Most funeral homes insist on using them, but they may or may not be required by state law.

Graveside services are formal memorial services conducted at the cemetery or at the designated burial site.

The **Great Rite** is a form of the *heiros gamos*, the sacred marriage of the Goddess and God, recreated most commonly in ritual by the Priestess' blessing with her athame of the sacramental wine her Priest holds for her. On special occasions, the Great Rite is enacted physically—and privately—by a Priestess and Priest who are bonded. It isn't the same thing that you see in movies. It's like the lightning quickening the primal seas, and Witches call it holy.

Handfasting is a Wiccan ritual by which lovers are bound in the equivalent of matrimony. The marriage can be religious only, but it is often legal as well.

The **inner** is another name for the personal (often private) astral planes.

Your **inner child** is the little kid you used to be, the one that got confused and blamed when you grew up the first time. Your inner child is also the archetypal Divine Child, your sense of wonder and trust and glory. You can re-raise your inner child so as to deal with your past in practical psychological terms and reclaim the spiritual energy your child's been holding for you. Look at John Bradshaw's book, listed in the Bibliography.

Interment is the act of burying a body or ashes.

The **Inquisition** was the European Church's campaign against heresy—a word which comes from the ancient Greek for *choice*—that lasted roughly 400 years and decimated Europe. Our lore speaks of 9 million Europeans (mostly women) who were "executed," most of them burned, which is why that period is also called the Burning Times.

Karma is a word and concept that Westerners have borrowed from the East. It's generally understood this way: if you do something lousy, something lousy will happen back to you. We think this is unreasonable, and not the way the Universe works. Adventure Wicca's interpretation is that if you do something lousy, you're demonstrating a need to improve your understanding, and the God/dess will meet that need through your experience. That *doesn't* mean, as it was put in the 1970s, that "God will get you for that." It means that you'll come upon an opportunity to learn what you need to. If you hurt somebody, you might as easily find yourself taking a first-aid class or assisting in an emergency as find yourself being injured.

Litha is the name of the Summer Solstice, one of eight Wiccan Sabbats in the year. Many of us pronounce it *'lee-ha* rather than *'leeth-ha*.

Magic is non-ordinary activity or experience. You can *work* magic, you can *witness* magic, you can *feel* it around or nearby. It ranges in "size" and "shape" from love to ritual, from personal to local (or regional or global or universal), from human to Gaian. It can be large or small, and while it certainly includes the candle, cord, rune and other magic we do in our Circles, it's equally certainly not limited to that. In its broadest sense, magic is anything that amazes or delights you, meets a need beyond ordinary meeting, or makes you "cry for happy." When I spell it with a *k*, magick, I'm talking about more ceremonial models and approaches than Wiccans usually take.

A **marker** is a monument or memorial—a grave stone, a boulder, a plaque or anything else that marks the place (or designated place) of burial.

A **medicine wheel** is an American Indian form of communication with the gods and spirits, a device of evocation and invocation. The glossary in Brooke Medicine Eagle's *White Buffalo Woman Comes Singing* (Ballantine Books, New York, 1991) says that it's "a symbolic wheel of life containing all directions, attributes, aspects, things, and beings. The stone circles which portray this symbolism are sometimes laid out in alignment with the sun at the solstices, or with other astrological events."

A **memorial service**, in conventional parlance, is a funeral service at which the body is not present (but at which ashes or other mementos or tokens may be).

A **mausoleum** is a building where coffins can be interred above the ground. (See **entombment**.)

The **mortician** is the person who's in charge of preparing a body for disposition. (See **funeral director**.)

A **mortuary** is a funeral home. Dead bodies are prepared for disposition here, and that can mean anything from quick dressing and arrangement in a casket for direct burial or cremation to embalming the body in preparation for viewing or an open-casket service.

Mundane is something performed or perceived or experienced as unmagical, ordinary, everyday, material, practical, secular. (Any of which things can be made magical.)

A **niche** is the shelf or recess in a columbarium where containers of ashes are set. Some of them have glass fronts so you can see the urn inside, others have solid fronts to which identifying plaques are attached. Some of them have holders for live or artificial flowers, which you can bring yourself or pay to have maintained.

An **obituary** is a brief notice of death in the paper. It usually includes the name and age of the person who has died, and usually names the funeral establishment as well so that people who read the obituary can call and ask about services and where memorial donations should be sent; sometimes that information is included in the published death notice.

Pagan comes from the Latin *pagani*, which means *country dweller*. It means *non-Christian* now because according to our lore, the country folk were the last to be converted to Christianity in Europe and Britain.

Paleo- is a prefix meaning *ancient,* as in stone-age, long ago, cave-painting time and before.

Passages are significant transitions. They can be biological (birthdays, hormones, death), geographical, emotional, social, political, etc., especially when they are archetypal and universal. Any transition or aspect of transition that is important to the individual in transit is a Passage.

Perfect love and perfect trust is an idea, a goal, a metaphor, and an expression of feeling safe as a part of nature. This implies not only that *Nature* is okay, but that being *part* of things, rather than dominant over them, is okay, too. It is an attitude that Wiccans choose to take, and it doesn't mean we're gullible. It does mean realizing that your worth doesn't always depend on your individuality and that giving yourself up to the Whole is safe.

A **pre-need plan** (which may also be referred to as **the pre-arrangements**) is a collection of decisions and information made prior to death so that mourners don't have to take care of so many of the details.

A **quest** is a mission, a calling. It doesn't have to be organized, it doesn't even have to be very well defined. It can even be something you keep finding yourself doing in different ways, rather than something you know you're setting out to do. It becomes a capital-Q Quest when you recognize and acknowledge and accept it.

Rebirthing is a psycho-spiritual process by which we cast off the unsatisfactory persona we've been assigned or have stumbled into without design, to deliberately become the person we feel we really are. This is often a long and personal process, and it can be recognized and symbolized and affirmed ritually, as it is in a Wiccan Initiation.

The **Rede** or Wiccan Rede is simple: *An ye harm none, do as ye will.*

Refrigeration is a temporary means of preserving a dead body.

Reincarnation is the process of re-embodying personality-energy, and an endless cycle. Nobody knows exactly how it works with people, but we see lots of examples of life returning from death in the natural world, and it's an ancient and unbroken human conviction that *we* come back from death into other lives, too.

Ritual is choreographed and/or scripted/memorized (or spontaneous within a consistent framework) worship, ranging from almost standard liturgical material to reverent personal habits. Rituals usually include some form of chant or song and some form of dance or other movement. Its purpose is to help a worshiper open up to God/dess energy, perception and experience.

The **Rollright Ritual** is a great (and complex) ritual to restore us to our proper relationship with rocks, which represent far more than their mere mineral content and mundane uses. I read about it in William Gray's *By Standing Stone & Elder Tree: Ritual & the Unconscious*, published in 1990 by Llewellyn. The Rollright Ritual emphasizes rebirth.

Sabbats are the eight solar holidays on the Wiccan calendar, which is called the Wheel of the Year. They include the two solstices and the two equinoxes and four Cross-Quarter days: February 1 or 2, April 30/May 1, August 1 or 2 and October 31/November 1. These holidays mark the course of mortal life through its cycle.

Suicide literally means self-death. It refers to an intentional act, but not to predictable consequences or carelessness, although common parlance may say something like, "So and So committed suicide with all that stress."

The **Summerland** is an astral "place" where our souls rest between incarnations. It encompasses the Underworld, several astral planes, and a variety of states of mind and being. There we review what we learned in our most recent life and prepare for the next, or at least that's how we talk about the sort of experience we expect.

Thealogy is the study of Goddess and the relationships between God/dess and humanity; and the study of Wiccan and other Pagan philosophies and issues. Similar to *theology*, but having to do with a generative principle that is feminine rather than masculine and proceeding from correspondingly different premises.

A **Traditional service** is, in the mainstream, a religious funeral at which the body is present. Your own Wiccan tradition may have a standard requiem, but if you're talking about that when you say "traditional service" to anyone outside the Craft, you'll be misunderstood.

The **Underworld** is an aspect of the astral, an aspect of the Summerland. Different corners of its realms and levels are known in every culture. It's called the Underworld, not because it's really "under" anything physical, but because it was named when people believed as a matter of physics in an overhead realm of gods and an underground realm of the dead. It's appropriate psychologically too, of course, for it refers to the realms that underlie our conscious experience and perception.

An **urn** is a commonly used container for cremains. Urns are made of various materials including wood, marble, or metal. Urns are not, however, the only sorts of containers in which ashes may be kept. For Wiccans, pouches work very well, and many people use boxes too. (I rather like wood, in any shape, because wood can be carved or burned with the initials of the deceased, or with other phrases or symbols that are appropriate. Metal and stone containers can also be personalized, but wood is easier for most of us to work with.)

Viewing is as much a process as an act: the body, in an open casket, is secluded in a quiet room, usually at a funeral parlor, and during certain designated times, friends and family are invited to come and pay their last respects. For mourners, this can mean anything from signing the book and peeking to spending quite some time talking to the body or meditating nearby. Sometimes, family members sit with the body and a group of friends gather; sometimes the room is mostly empty.

Wicca is what we call the modern re-creation of Native (Western European) Anglo-Norman-Saxon-Celtic tradition of Witchcraft. Wicca experiences deity as a complimentary polarity. Wiccans worship according to the cycles of the Moon and Sun. With roots in paleo-European cave culture, modern Wicca is a synthesis of many Indo-European and Romano-Celtic traditions and is composed of several Traditions or "denominations."

Wiccan scripture is Nature. Everything from watching the squirrels bury nuts in the park to astrophysics—natural history and how it happens; the Natural model. Wicca has no ultimate Book of Authority, but there are some good shows on PBS and cable, and every Witch has a personal Book of Shadows.

Widdershins is an anti-Sunwise (counterclockwise) direction of travel. (See **deosil**.)

Witch may refer to Wiccans or to other Anglo-Celtic or European followers of the Craft. It comes from the Anglo-Saxon (Old English) words *wicce* and *wicca* (feminine and masculine, pronounced *wee-cheh* and *wee-chah* respectively). The root, *wic*, means *bend* or *shape*; Witches are the ones who *do* the bending or shaping, not the ones who get bent or shaped (by evil delusions, motives or beings, some would say; they're wrong). Over the centuries the focus of pronunciation in English has changed and the old gender distinctions have disappeared; the modern word *witch* refers to both men and women.

Zero-sum is economist Lester Thurow's description of the economy in terms of a finite amount of *X*, which means that if I have a lot, you can only have a little. For me to win, you have to lose. It's the economic version of *either/or*.

Bibliography

Adams, Douglas. *The Hitchhiker's Guide to the Galaxy.* Simon & Schuster, Pocket Books, New York, 1979, 1985.

Bates, Brian. *The Way of Wyrd.* Century Publishing, London, 1983.

Beyerl, Paul V. *A Wiccan Bardo.* Prism-Unity, Prism Press, Dorset, 1989.

Bosworth, Joseph, and T. Northcote Toller. *An Anglo-Saxon Dictionary.* Oxford University Press, London, 1898, 1964.

Bradshaw, John. *Homecoming: Reclaiming and Championing Your Inner Child.* Bantam Books, New York, 1990.

Buckland, Raymond. *Buckland's Complete Book of Witchcraft.* Llewellyn Publishing, St. Paul, 1986.

Campbell, Joseph. *Historical Atlas of World Mythology,* Vol. I, Part I. Perennial Library, Harper & Row, New York, 1988.

———. *The Inner Reaches of Outer Space.* Perennial Library, Harper & Row, New York, 1986.

———. *The Masks of God: Creative Mythology.* Penguin Books, New York, 1968.

———, ed. *The Portable Jung.* Translated by R.F.C. Hull. Penguin Books, New York, 1976.

Capra, Fritjof. *The Tao of Physics.* Bantam Books, New York, 1984.

Castaneda, Carlos. *The Teachings of Don Juan: A Yaqui Way of Knowledge.* University of California Press, Berkeley, 1968.

Clark, W. G., and W. Aldis Wright, eds. *The Complete Works of William Shakespeare.* Nelson Doubleday, Inc., New York (Book Club edition).

Duda, Deborah. *A Guide to Dying at Home.* John Muir Publications, Santa Fe, New Mexico, 1982.

Dungan, Christine K. *The Impact of Varied Religious Traditions on the Approach of Clergy to Death and Dying: Four Personal Reflections.* Spring, 1985 (unpublished paper).

Farrar, Janet, and Stewart. *A Witches Bible Compleat,* combined Volumes I and II. Magickal Childe Publishing, New York, 1981, 1984.

Foos-Graber, Anya. *Deathing*. Nicholas-Hays, Inc., York Beach, Maine, 1989.

Forward, Susan, with Craig Buck. *Toxic Parents: Overcoming Their Hurtful Legacy and Reclaiming Your Life*. Bantam Books, New York, 1989.

Fremantle, Francesca, and Chögyam Trungpa, trans. *The Tibetan Book of the Dead, the Great Liberation Through Hearing in the Bardo*. Shambhala, Boulder & London, 1975.

Gardner, Gerald. *The Meaning of Witchcraft*. Magickal Childe, Inc., New York, 1988.

———. *Witchcraft Today*. Magickal Childe, Inc., New York, 1988.

Gray, William. *By Standing Stone and Elder Tree*. Llewellyn, St. Paul, 1990.

Harner, Michael. *The Way of the Shaman*. Bantam Books, New York, 1982.

Hobbes, Thomas. *Leviathan: or matter, forme and power of a commonwealth ecclesiastical and civil*. Edited by Michael Oakeshott. Collier Books, New York, 1962.

Humphrey, Derek. *Final Exit*. The Hemlock Society, Los Angeles, 1991.

Jacobi, Jolande. *The Psychology of C. G. Jung*. Yale University Press, New Haven and London, 1962, 1968.

Jung, Emma, and Marie-Louise Von Franz. *The Grail Legend*. Translated by Andrea Dykes. Sigo Press, Boston, 1986.

Kavanaugh, Robert E. *Facing Death*. Penguin Books, 1972.

Keyes, Ken Jr. *The Hundredth Monkey*. Vision Books, St. Mary, Kentucky, 1981.

Kübler-Ross, Elisabeth. *Death, the Final Stage of Growth*. Touchstone Books, Simon & Schuster, New York, 1975.

———. *On Death and Dying*. Collier Books, MacMillan Publishing Co., New York, 1969.

Lewis, C. S. *The Chronicles of Narnia*. Collier Books, New York, 1970.

———. *The Great Divorce*. MacMillan, New York, 1946.

MacLaine, Shirley. *Out on a Limb*. Bantam Books, New York, 1983.

Mariechild, Diane. *Mother Wit*. The Crossing Press, Freedom, California, 1981.

McAleer, Neil. *The Body Almanac*. Doubleday & Co., Garden City, 1985.

Medicine Eagle, Brooke. *Buffalo Woman Comes Singing*. Ballantine Books, New York, 1991.

Milford, Jessica. *The American Way of Death*. Simon & Schuster, New York, 1963.

Moody, Raymond A. Jr., M.D. *Life After Life*. Bantam Books, New York, 1975.

Moore, Robert, and Douglas Gillette. *King, Warrior, Magician, Lover, Rediscovering the Archetypes of the Mature Masculine.* HarperSanFrancisco, 1990.

Peck, M. Scott, M.D. *People of the Lie: The Hope for Healing Human Evil.* Touchstone Books, Simon & Schuster, New York, 1983.

————. *The Different Drum.* Touchstone Books, Simon & Schuster, New York, 1987.

Peterson, Roger Tory. *A Field Guide to Western Birds.* Houghton-Mifflin Company, Boston, 1961.

Putman, John. "The Search for Modern Humans," in *National Geographic*, Oct. 1988.

Sagan, Carl. *The Dragons of Eden.* Random House, New York, 1977.

Starhawk. *The Spiral Dance, a Rebirth of the Ancient Religion of the Great Goddess.* 10th anniversary ed. HarperSanFrancisco, 1989.

————. *Dreaming the Dark: Magic, Sex and Politics.* Beacon Press, Boston, 1982, 1988.

————. *Truth or Dare: Encounters with Power, Authority and Mystery.* Harper & Row, San Francisco, 1987.

————, and M. Macha Nightmare and the Reclaiming Collective. *The Pagan Book of Living and Dying.* HarperSanFrancisco, 1997.

Stein, Diane. *Stroking the Python: Women's Psychic Lives.* Llewellyn Publications, St. Paul, 1988.

Strong, Maggie. *Mainstay, for the Well Spouse of the Chronically Ill.* Penguin Books, New York, 1988.

Thurow, Lester C. *The Zero-Sum Society, Distribution and the Possibilities for Economic Change.* Penguin Books, New York, 1981.

Ward, Geoffrey C., with Ric Burns and Ken Burns. *The Civil War: an illustrated history.* Borzoi Books, Alfred A. Knopf, New York, 1990.

Warren-Clarke, Ly. *The Way of the Goddess.* Prism-Unity, Prism Press, Dorset, 1987.

Webster's New World Dictionary of the American Language. World Publishing Co., Cleveland and New York, 1962.

Wiesel, Elie. "The Death of My Father," in *Jewish Reflections on Death.* Schocken Books, New York, 1974.

Weissenberg, Debbie A. *You'll Never Walk Alone: Hospital Survival Techniques.* Whitewing Press, San Francisco, 1998. For copies contact Fran Weissenberg, Post Office Box 57070, Tucson, AZ 85732.

Index